TEACHING TI

MW00768235

# TEACHING THE AMERICAN REVOLUTION THROUGH PLAY

CHRISTOPHER HARRIS AND PATRICIA HARRIS, Ph.D., WITH BRIAN MAYER

Rosen Classroom
PROFESSIONAL RESOURCES™

Rosen Classroom

Published in 2015 by The Rosen Publishing Group, Inc.
29 East 21st Street, New York, NY 10010

First Edition

### Cataloging-in-Publication Data

Harris, Christopher.
Teaching the American Revolution through play/by Christopher Harris, Patricia Harris, PhD, and Brian Mayer.
p. cm. — (Teaching through games)
Includes appendix.
ISBN 978-1-4994-9004-6 (paperback)
1. United States — History — Revolution, 1775 - 1783 — Study and teaching — Activity programs. 2. United States — History — Revolution, 1775 - 1783 — Study and teaching. 3. Teaching — Aids and devices. I. Harris, Christopher, 1977-. II. Harris, Patricia. III. Mayer, Brian. IV. Title.
E208.H37 2015
973.3—d23

Manufactured in the United States of America

Code Word: forliberty

Use the code word above to register for an account on the series website at http://teachingthroughgames.com. Or, if you have already registered, use the code to add this book to your existing account. The website contains the readings and sheets referenced in this book as well as additional game elements. There is also a discussion forum where you can share successful practices and ask questions.

**Photo Credits:** cover (statue) © Dennis Hammer/www.istockphoto.com; cover (map) © Getty Images; cover, pp. i, 70 (cannon) © Braddo/ www.istockphoto.com; pp. i, 70 cannon ball © Dutch Scenery/www.istockphoto.com; p. iv © Universal Images Group /Getty Images; pp. viii, 2 © www.academygames.com; p. 39 © De Agostini Picture Library/Getty Images.

# CONTENTS

Introduction   iv
  Re-Learning History   v
  The Importance of War Games   vi
  A Play-Based Approach to the
    American Revolution   viii

**Lesson 1: Rebellion in the Colonies**
**Teaching with 1775: Rebellion**   2
  Lesson Plan: Was the colonial victory
    in the American Revolution
    inevitable?   6

**Lesson 2: Taxation Without**
**Representation**   9
  Historical Information   9
  Lesson Plan: Why did taxation
    without representation anger the
    colonists so much and how is it
    related to the idea of
    self-governance?   15
  Primary Source Document: From
    "The Examination of Doctor
    Franklin"   15

**Lesson 3: Rising Hostilities**   27
  Historical Information   27
  Lesson Plan: What was the cause of
    escalating hostilities before the start
    of the Revolutionary War?   30
  Primary Source Document: "Case
    of Capt. Thomas Preston"   34
  Primary Source Document: "The
    Bloody Massacre" (engraving)   38

**Lesson 4: The War Before the**
**Declaration**   40
  Historical Information   40
  Lesson Plan: What are the many
    factors of war that can determine
    the outcome?   45

**Lesson 5: Independence Declared and**
**Gained**   50
  Historical Information   50
  Lesson Plan: Why might a revolution
    end in independence, and why
    might it not?   58
  Primary Source Document: "Alphabet
    for Little Masters and Misses"   58

Notes   64

Appendix 1   66
  Common Core Learning
    Standards
  Social Studies Standards

Appendix 2   69
  Important Details Worksheet   70

About the Authors   71

# INTRODUCTION

# RE-LEARNING HISTORY

The first time I saw Beau Beckett and Jeph Stahl's board game 1775: Rebellion (Academy Games, 2013), I asked the publisher about the name. The American Revolution was linked in my mind with the 1776 Declaration of Independence. Yet the initial battles of the war in Lexington and Concord, Massachusetts, happened on April 19, 1775. In the winter of 1775, the American Continental Army even went on the offensive invading Canada to capture Montreal and lay siege to Quebec. It wasn't until after newly promoted General George Washington drove British forces out of Boston in early 1776 that the Continental Congress could secure enough votes for the formal Declaration of Independence ratified on July 4, 1776.

It was through playing 1775 that I rediscovered the history of early America that I had either forgotten or never really learned. The American Revolution and colonial struggle for independence was more than just the Boston Tea Party, Paul Revere's Ride, and Valley Forge. This was an international conflict, a war of proxies extending centuries old conflicts involving the imperial powers of Europe. The American Revolution was just another front for the British army already stretched thin by an ongoing war with France and Spain. The game reminds us of this with the inclusion of both French forces and the Hessian (German) mercenaries hired by the British to bolster their troops.

The game's mechanics also point out another often overlooked fact of history, not everyone in the colonies wanted independence from Britain. The game handles up to four players, two on each side of the conflict. One player from each team controls the British army or the Continental Army, the other the English Loyalists or the Patriot militias. Native American forces are also represented as independent forces that were recruited and used by both sides. With a map that ranges from Georgia through Quebec and Nova Scotia, players get a sense of the vast scale of a war that ranged from early Canadian invasions to the southern most colonies. Gameplay and the lesson resources included here are aligned to content typically taught in seventh grade, tenth grade, and AP American History in many states.

## THE IMPORTANCE OF WAR GAMES

In 1954, less than 200 years after the American Revolution, the United States once again found itself at the center of world politics—this time as a lead force in the Cold War as opposed to a proxy colony in the ongoing Anglo-French wars. In 1954, America was once again divided, this time by the constant stream of unsubstantiated allegations of Senator McCarthy and his Communist witch hunts. President Eisenhower warned of the domino theory as tensions rose in Vietnam following the very uncertain end of the Korean War only a year earlier. Amid all of this insecurity, The RAND Corporation was tapped to investigate the effectiveness of analog gaming as a way to increase analysis and situational understanding within the U.S. military. This isn't, authors Mood and Specht are quick to point out, an issue of war-gaming, but rather concerns the general importance of a game-based approach to understanding.

> *Our example, the American Kriegsspiel [a post–Civil War war game developed by the Rhode Island militia], has illustrated the more or less traditional use of the human computer as employed in a war game. This use of gaming can be extended to those non-military situations that involve elements of conflict too important to be ignored. That is, gaming may be used to study situations in which there are elements having a significant effect but which are in the control of a competitor or opponent.*[1]

As Mood and Specht considered the nascent computers available in 1954, the computing power that could be imbued in an analog rule-set was far preferable. Even though our modern computing power has far exceeded anything that might have been imagined in 1954, analog gaming is still a powerful tool for learning.

Mood and Specht focus on the process of designing a quality game; it involves a huge number of factors and questions that must be addressed. By working through all of these issues, the game represents the expert understanding of many different people. That understanding is also structured by the game to help guide outcomes and analysis of a problem.

> *The human decision link in our machine is not free but rather is bound by all the constraints of the machine, constraints that express the structure of the model and that have been arrived at by combing the knowledge and experience of many experts. So, while irrational play may be present in either the gaming solution of a problem or in a solution arrived at by a round-table discussion among experts, the gaming technique does have some built in safeguards.*[2]

Despite the incredible advances in computer technology and artificial intelligence, computer programs are still relatively limited by what was initially coded. If the programmers didn't think about a possible solution, the program may not be set up to handle it. Given the increased openness possible when humans bring natural flexibility to the implementation of an analog rule set as opposed to the rigidness of a computer, games are an especially powerful way to explore historical and military scenarios. Though the constraints Mood and Specht refer to in an expertly designed game guide players toward better decisions, board games still allow humans to be creative.

Playing 1775 lets learners explore and interact within the historical context of the American colonies' efforts to gain freedom from England. Constraints are presented within the rules to limit movement and combat interactions, but in a simplified way that allows players to spend more time focusing on analysis and decision making as opposed to fiddling with markers in a war game. To extend the learning, this resource also presents a custom designed game, Intolerable Acts, that helps learners explore the politics that led to the American Revolution. The game presents guidelines for responses by players in the form of character sheets that explain each figure's thoughts and personal goals. There are constraints, but players will also be free to

re-create history to find new solutions — or more drastic failures — that could have happened had things gone but a little bit differently.

# A PLAY-BASED APPROACH TO THE AMERICAN REVOLUTION

This resource presents a one-week unit for teaching the American Revolution. The five lessons cover the political events leading up to the war, major battles from the war itself, and the aftermath and initial formation of the United States of America. To introduce the topic, we are jumping right into the thick of things by using 1775: Rebellion to explore the war itself. By starting with the end result, learners can use the map and events of the game to gain a high-level overview of the locations, people, and politics that will be discussed in later lessons.

The next two lessons will jump back in time to the years before the revolution to review how and why relations between England and the colonies deteriorated. To support a deeper investigation into the complexities of the situation in the colonies in this period, we have also designed a new game scenario, Intolerable Acts, to engage players in a social/historical experience. Drawing from key figures from the period, players will work in teams to navigate through the complexities of the situation as they try to meet individual goals for England, the American colonies, and France and other European nations.

The fourth lesson will cover the war years, again referring back to 1775 for context and analysis of the progression of battles. In the final lesson, we will consider the implications of independence, both the Declaration of Independence itself and the process of actually forming a new nation. Though England lost both the war and the American colonies, this was actually one of the best things that could have happened for its empire.

# LESSON 1: REBELLION IN THE COLONIES

*Listen, my children, and you shall hear*
*Of the midnight ride of Paul Revere,*
*On the eighteenth of April, in Seventy-Five…*
— Henry Wadsworth Longfellow[3]

The date is right there in Longfellow's famous poem 1775. Yet the 1776 signing of the Declaration of Independence is so overpowering in our understanding of American history that we often forget that the colonists had been fighting the Revolutionary War for more than a year before the Declaration was signed. Tensions had been rising for years as a series of taxes and acts imposed on the colonies by the British Parliament increasingly angered the American colonies. Though the concept of fighting for independence remained anathema for some, by early 1775 many colonists were ready to fight. On April 18, 1775, British forces from Boston headed toward Lexington and Concord to arrest leaders of the rebellion in Massachusetts and destroy supplies. Warned by Paul Revere—and the lesser known William Dawes and Samuel Prescott, the latter being the only one who actually completed the midnight ride to Concord—more than 500 militiamen met the British Regulars in Concord on April 19 and turned them back. The militia's continued ambushes and small attacks as the British retreated to Boston inflicted light losses but delivered a serious message to the British army. British general Hugh Percy later wrote that the colonial militia "attacked us in a very scattered, irregular manner, but with perseverance and resolution…Whoever looks upon them as an irregular mob, will find himself very much mistaken."[4] It was April 1775, and war had begun.

# TEACHING WITH 1775: REBELLION

As a historical war game, 1775: Rebellion attempts to accurately portray the political and military situation during the American Revolution. Though the game allows for different outcomes based on both chance and the strategic choices of the players, the initial setup is historically correct. This means you can start teaching about the American Revolution from the first moment that the game box is shared with learners. For example, consider the cover of the box; what might we infer from the picture?

The British forces in their eponymous red coats are advancing in formation against a motley group of individuals hiding behind trees. Though one of the colonists is dressed in the blue of the Continental Army, the other two fighters depicted seem to be irregular, militia forces. It was this type of militia ambush that so demoralized the British on their retreat from the first battles at Lexington and Concord, a strategy that would serve the colonial forces well throughout the war.

The initial setup of the game board also presents a great deal of information for us to analyze. We think of the Revolutionary War as taking place in the Middle Atlantic States from Massachusetts to Virginia, but the map ranges from Georgia to the maritime provinces of Canada, British holdings after the end of the French and Indian War. In fact, during the first Continental Army push of the war in late 1775, American forces captured Montreal and laid siege to Quebec. Consider also the initial deployment of British and colonial forces. The Continental Army, the formal forces of the colonies, are represented by blue cubes, and colonial militia forces as white cubes. At the start of the war, British forces hold Boston, New York City, Philadelphia, and New Jersey. It is critical to note that the British forces include regular army troops, red coats represented by red cubes, and loyalist militia forces represented by yellow cubes. As we will see in later lessons, a large portion of colonists remained loyal to England. In many ways, this was as much a civil war as a revolutionary war.

## PHASES OF GAMEPLAY

1775: Rebellion presents a greatly simplified rule set that preserves the strategic elements of a war game while also adding enough chance to support players of different skill levels. The game plays across a number of rounds—at least three, but the actual number will be determined by conditions within the game—with each of the four factions taking their turns in random order based on drawing a cube from a bag. A player's turn consists of four phases:

### Reinforcements Phase

At the start of each turn, a player receives four reinforcement cubes from his or her stockpile as well as any additional cubes from his or her faction that are in the fled troops box. However, these troops can only be placed into a city area within a colony controlled by that side. If your side doesn't control a colony, then no new troops or fled troops are placed. Colony control is thus very important, not only for your score but also as a way to ensure reinforcements.

3

## Movement Phase

During this second phase, a player must play one, and only one, movement card from their hand. Note that this might force a player to prematurely play a truce card (considered a movement card) that could end the war to his or her detriment.

Army movement is easy; a movement card will show how many armies can be moved and how many spaces each army can move. The tricky part is the definition of an army. In 1775, an army is a collection of cubes where each cube represents a particular unit in the army. An army can consist of multiple types of troops from the same side—for example, red cubes for British Regulars and yellow cubes for Loyalist militia as well as green cubes representing aligned Native Americans. For movement, the whole army can move together, or a part of the army can split off to move. There are two important movement rules to remember: first, no army or individual unit (cube) can be moved more than once a turn; second, you can only move armies containing at least one cube from your faction. If you are playing as the Loyalist militia, you cannot move an army that has only British Regulars in it.

Movement cards refer to either land movement or water movement and indicate the number of armies to be moved by showing a number of soldiers. Thus, a movement card that shows three soldier figures means that three armies (each consisting of any number of units) can be moved. The restriction to this is that some militia water movement cards involve smaller fishing boats that can handle only three units at a time. Players can also play up to two event cards in this phase or the battle phase. The event cards will indicate when they can be played.

## Battle Phase

Battle in 1775: Rebellion is handled with dice rolls. Defenders act first, rolling one die of the appropriate color for each cube involved in the battle. After resolving the defender dice results, the attackers roll their dice. Each faction rolls their own dice, so even though it may be the

4

turn of the player controlling the British Regulars, the Loyalist militia player rolls his or her own dice if any yellow cubes are involved in the combat. Dice results are simple. A bullseye represents a hit and the opposing forces have to remove one cube from the battle and return it to the appropriate stockpile for each bullseye rolled. The lost unit can come from any of the involved forces as decided together by the players controlling them. Most dice also have a fleeing figure. For each flee result, a player must move one of his or her own cubes into the fled units box. Note that the dice for the British red coats and the French forces, two professional armies filled with veterans from near constant fighting over previous decades, do not have a flee face. After resolving hits and fleeing units, the last type of roll is handled. A blank die face is called a command decision; for each blank face rolled the player may decide to have one of his or her unit cubes retreat to an adjacent region without enemy forces. Players will want to carefully consider the faces on their faction's dice when considering the deployment of forces and handling losses in battle. Regular troops have a higher percentage of faces with hits as compared to militia.

## Draw Cards Phase

During the final phase in a player's turn, he or she draws back up to three cards. If, after drawing, a player does not have a movement card in hand, he or she reveals the hand and then shuffles the cards back in to the remaining deck and draws again. A player must have a movement card in his or her hand. Note that the truce cards are considered movement cards for this rule and the must play rule.

## Game End

The game ends when, after round three, either the two British factions or the two American factions (or both factions on both sides) have each played their Treaty of Paris truce cards. For example, if both the British Regulars and the Loyalist militia players have both played their truce cards—by choice, or through being forced to play it as their only movement card—the game ends at the end of that round. Whichever side controls more colonies wins. In the case of a tie, the rules note quite cheekily, consider the American colonies to have become a new providence of a rebuilt French Canada.

## Game Modification

1775: Rebellion is designed for two teams, and so works best as a four-player game. However, especially for our intended use of the game as an instructional tool to introduce the war and inspire interest and discussion in this first lesson, the game can actually work very nicely with larger groups. With two to four players discussing and planning the moves for each faction, players will have more opportunities to reflect on the historical aspects of the game.

# LESSON PLAN

## Essential Question

Was the colonial victory in the American Revolution inevitable?

## Game Lesson

Introduce the game and game vocabulary. Use the game board as a focal point for introducing the game components to the students.

The following concepts are important to understanding the game and mechanisms needed to play.

- Reinforcements
- Hessians
- Mercenaries
- Regulars
- Militia
- Patriots
- Loyalists

The game box can provide clues about the game before we even open it. As noted in the previous paragraphs, the cover depicts a common type of encounter from the war—Patriot militiamen hiding in the woods are ambushing British Regulars. What more can we tell from examining the board, cards, and other resources?

## GUIDED PRACTICE

To prepare students for success while playing 1775: Rebellion, it will help to review how armies move and how battles are fought before the first game. Movement and battle actions are described previously and are also illustrated nicely in the rulebook. To model how the game works, you might consider setting up some cubes on the board to demonstrate a single turn of movement and battle.

## INDEPENDENT PRACTICE

Have students play at least a few turns—or a whole game depending on time available—and then discuss the following:

- Did you have a strategy as the game started?
- Did you feel that your side, or the other side, had the advantage? Why? What specific actions did you or the other side take that were most successful?
- When you play again, what actions will you change to be more successful?

### Writing Activities

If you are planning on using these writing activities, it may help to have students keep some notes during gameplay to help them in their later writing.

**Narrative:** Many of the soldiers kept diaries. Write three to five brief entries in a diary format that tell the story of a soldier in one of the units in the game. Where did he march? Where did he fight? What happened?

**Inform or Explain:** Write a brief account of a battle from the game you just played that might have been published in a newspaper of the time. Be sure to include some background information on where the armies came from as well as the outcome and aftermath of the battle.

**Express an Opinion:** Modern conflicts are fought as much on Twitter as on the battlefield. Write ten short tweets that might have been sent by either a Patriot or Loyalist militiaman to report back on the progress of the war. Remember that these tweets are often very biased, inflammatory statements meant to sway opinion.

## SHARING/REFLECTION

Have students share their writing. Also, use this as a chance to reflect and discuss the importance of strategic thinking in games of this type. Additional times playing the game will help students begin to think more strategically about army movement and battle plans.

## ASSESSMENT

Assessment will consist of watching students play the game and reading their reflections on the experience and the gameplay. The writing activities are designed to engage students in the game and so may not accurately reflect history.

## EXTENSION ACTIVITIES

**Important Details:** Have students identify ten important details to know and justify their choices of those details using Important Details sheet in the appendix and available online at www.teachingthroughgames.com for printing. Answers will vary.

# LESSON 2: TAXATION WITHOUT REPRESENTATION

Great Britain and the English colonies in America had an uneasy relationship well before the American Revolution began. The distance between the sovereign power and the colonies was great. Some of the colonies were set up under charters with stock companies and those companies and the king appointed governors, so the legal authority was not vested in a person elected by the colonists. One might say that the underlying factors that led to rebellion began almost from the founding of the first colonies in 1607. The structure of governance from the beginning led to governance without representation for the colonists.

## HISTORICAL INFORMATION

The issue of no representation in Parliament moved into prominence after the Seven Years' War that Britain fought against both France and Spain for control of colonies and colonial trade. The North American front of the Seven Years' War is referred to as the French and Indian War. At the end of the war in 1763, Britain was devastated by war debt and Parliament felt that the colonies should be financially responsible for paying for their defense. Parliament passed several acts to introduce new taxes on the colonists. In British tradition, British citizens could only be taxed because they were represented in Parliament. Many of the colonists, who were not represented in Parliament, felt that they were being illegally taxed without representation. The initial outcry was not, as one might think, over the taxes themselves, which were actually relatively low, but over the idea that the colonies were being taxed without representation.

## THE FRENCH AND INDIAN WAR

The French and Indian War was the North American front of the larger Seven Years' War that saw Britain aligned with others against France and Spain for the control of colonies and trade routes. At the beginning of the war effort in North America, the British lost some major confrontations with the French, who were allied with the native population. It wasn't until William Pitt saw the need to involve the colonists to a greater degree and paid for colonial troops that the war effort turned around.

While it can be said that Britain won the war because of the gains in colonial power that they gained in North America and other places, at the end of the war in 1763, Britain was devastated by war debt. It was felt strongly in Britain that the costs of war should in part be recovered from colonies with additional taxes. Furthermore, Parliament decided that the British army that was housed in the colonies for ongoing defense should also be paid for through taxes on colonial trade.

## TAXATION WITHOUT REPRESENTATION

While the first taxes that Parliament imposed on the colonies were generally reasonable in amount, the colonists objected because they felt the taxes violated their rights, as British citizens. As British citizens, they had the right according to law and tradition in Britain, to be taxed only if they were represented in Parliament. Without representation, the colonists maintained, they could not legally be taxed. Despite the protests, the British Parliament imposed a series of new taxes and limitations on the colonists over the next decade. Some of the major taxes and laws included the Sugar Act, the Currency Act, the Quartering Acts, the Stamp Act, the Townsend Acts, and the Tea Act.

### The Sugar Act of 1764

The Sugar Act of 1764 imposed a tax on sugar imported to the colonies but also made clear that the purpose of the act was to establish a tax, not just to regulate trade. George Grenville, the British prime minister, expected the Sugar Act to raise about £78,000 of the £200,000 it cost Britain to maintain an army in North America. This was not, then, an unreasonable tax; it actually charged half the tax rate of the Molasses Act of 1733 that it replaced. The response, however, was quite negative. The colonial economy was experiencing a decline after the war because merchants were not supplying all the British troops that they had during the war, but the merchants blamed the new tax for the economic downturn and objected to it on the basis of financial loss.

## The Currency Act of 1764

The Currency Act of 1764, while not a tax itself, was designed to allow Britain control of the currency in the colonies. The various colonies had been using paper currency for doing business and the Currency Act abolished that system, declaring that any colonial money could not be used for legal purposes. This meant that colonists would have to pay taxes using British currency. The act also stated that violations of custom laws would be heard in a naval court rather than a colonial civilian court. It was believed, and rightly so, that the naval courts would favor British interests.

## The Quartering Act of 1765

Another law that imposed sanctions on the colonies without being a direct tax was the Quartering Act of 1765. It demanded that the colonies provide housing and provisions for British troops remaining in the colonies after the French and Indian War had ended. The colonies had paid to house and feed British soldiers during the war, but the colonists felt that being forced to continue to bear the costs during peace was unreasonable. Compliance with the Quartering Act was generally avoided by most of the colonies but added to the discontentment in the colonies.

## The Stamp Act of 1765

The Stamp Act of 1765 was passed by Parliament as a more direct tax that could not be easily avoided as it impacted all documents produced in the colonies. All printed materials had to be produced using paper with an embossed revenue stamp—this included not just legal documents like land deeds and court proceedings, but any printed materials including newspapers, pamphlets, and even playing cards. Although the revenue was really never collected because of colonial action against its collectors, the act became a rallying point for colonial resistance around the issue of taxation without representation. It was in response to the Stamp Act of 1765 that the Sons of Liberty emerged as a growing movement for independence and the Virginia House of Burgesses issued the Virginia Resolves, a series of statements written by Patrick Henry that formally protested the Stamp Act.

Benjamin Franklin testified before the British House of Commons in 1766 regarding the colonial response to the Stamp Act. When asked about American thoughts regarding Britain before the tax issues started in 1763, Franklin stated that the general sentiment was quite positive.

> [Colonists] submitted willingly to the government of the Crown, and paid, in their courts, obedience to acts of Parliament. Numerous as the people are in the several old provinces they cost you nothing in forts, citadels, garrisons, or armies, to keep them in subjection. They were governed by this country at the expense only of a little pen, ink, and paper; they were led by a thread. They had not only a respect but an affection for Great Britain; for its laws, its customs, and manners, and even a fondness for its fashions, that greatly increased the commerce.[5]

With the passing of the Stamp Act and other laws, this feeling was, according to Franklin, "very much altered" by 1765. The difference with the Stamp Act was that it was an internal tax that was unavoidable.

> An external tax is a duty laid on commodities imported; that duty is added to the first cost and other charges on the commodity, and, when it is offered for sale, makes a part of the price. If the people do not like it at that price,

*they refuse it; they are not obliged to pay it. But an internal tax is forced from the people without their consent if not laid by their own representatives. The Stamp Act says we shall have no commerce, make no exchange of property with each other, neither purchase nor grant, nor recover debts; we shall neither marry nor make our wills, unless we pay such and such sums; and thus it is intended to extort our money from us or ruin us by the consequence of refusing to pay it.*[6]

When asked if colonists would submit and pay the tax, Franklin responded, "They will never do it, unless compelled by force of arms."

The Stamp Act was repealed in March of 1766 following strong colonial resistance, mob violence, and declining support in Britain for the tax. William Pitt—a noted member of the British Parliament and namesake for Pittsburgh, Pennsylvania—supported the colonial resistance of the Stamp Act. "I rejoice," he wrote to Grenville, "that America has resisted. Three millions of people, so dead to all the feelings of liberty as voluntarily to submit to be slaves, would have been fit instruments to make slaves of the rest."[7] The colonial unrest that grew in response to the Stamp Act will be explored in greater detail in lesson three.

### The Townshend Acts

The Townshend Acts, a series of laws proposed by Chancellor Charles Townshend, were passed after the repeal of the Stamp Act. The major taxes came from the Revenue Act of 1767, which placed duties on imports of glass, lead, paints, paper, and tea. These were, Townshend proposed, external taxes of the variety that Franklin had noted to be more acceptable. Colonists could, Townshend noted, simply not purchase the taxed items if they did not want to pay the tax. Townshend was, it would turn out, quite wrong. Americans, already angered over the Stamp Act, responded quite negatively and increasingly violently to the new taxes. In response, additional British troops were sent to Boston to protect custom commissioners from angry mobs. On March 5, 1770, after months of smaller clashes, the violence flared up in the Boston Massacre, where five colonists were killed after attacking and provoking a group of British soldiers. Coincidentally, it was on the same day that Parliament first took up action to repeal some of the Townshend Acts. The move to repeal was based on prior news of colonial unrest and a colonial boycott; Parliament would not learn of the Boston Massacre for some time due to communication delays.

## The Tea Act

In 1773, three years after the Boston Massacre and the repeal of the Townshend Acts, the British Parliament passed a new law that would once again anger the American colonies. The Tea Act imposed no new taxes, rather it allowed British agents to sell surplus tea owned by the British East India Company—a company indirectly controlled by the British government—at a bargain price by removing export duties. The intention in removing import/export costs was to undercut the tea prices offered by colonial merchants, many of who were selling smuggled Dutch tea. The Tea Act worked because the taxes on tea from the Townshend Acts were still in place.

The colonists saw this as just another scheme to force them to accept taxes without representation by establishing a monopoly on the tea trade designed to eliminate all other options. In response, many colonies refused to allow ships bringing tea to dock and unload their cargo. In some locations, colonists took things further by actively destroying the tea.

The most famous action to destroy tea came to be known as the Boston Tea Party. On December 16, 1773, members of the Sons of Liberty—a group led by Samuel Adams, though there is some question as to whether or not he planned or was involved in the Boston Tea Party—disguised themselves as Mohawk Native Americans, boarded three British ships, and dumped their tea into the Boston Harbor. Some colonial leaders, including Benjamin Franklin, worried that the Sons of Liberty had gone too far with the Boston Tea Party. Franklin, fearing a brutal response from the British army, encouraged repayment for the lost tea. Samuel Adams rejected this, calling Franklin a "bungling politician" and later boldly claiming that the "whole continent is now become united in sentiment and opposition to tyranny."[8]

As we will see, this was indeed quite an exaggerated claim. In early 1774, following the Boston Tea Party and only one year before the start of the war, most colonists, including many who we now remember as patriot leaders, still could not imagine independence from Britain. They were simply seeking fair treatment and representation.

## LESSON PLAN

### ESSENTIAL QUESTION

Why did taxation without representation anger the colonists so much and how is it related to the idea of self-governance?

### VOCABULARY

The following vocabulary words are important concepts for understanding the tax issues behind the American Revolution:
- Taxation
- Representation
- Quartering
- Indirect tax
- External tax
- Internal tax

### SUGGESTED READING RESOURCES

#### Primary Source Document

Excerpts from "The Examination of Doctor Franklin, before an August Assembly, relating to the Repeal of the Stamp-Act, &c." In 1766, Benjamin Franklin testified before the British House of Commons about the Stamp Act of 1765. This document is included after the lesson in an annotated form with vocabulary underlined and some important passages for close reading highlighted; it is available online at www.teachingthroughgames.com for printing.

An original printing of the testimony, and full transcript, can be found online at the Massachusetts Historical Society website.

### Other Sources

Chapter 1 from *The American Revolution and the Young Republic: 1763 to 1816*

Written by Britannica Educational Publishing

Published by Britannica Educational Publishing, 2011

ISBN: 9781615306688

*The American Revolutionary War and the War of 1812: People, Politics, and Power*

Written by Britannica Educational Publishing

Published by Britannica Educational Publishing, 2009

ISBN: 978615300228

## MINI READING LESSON

While you are reading the available primary source document or the suggested reading resources, attempt to answer the following question: Why was taxation without representation such an important issue for the colonies that it would lead to the American Revolution?

Introduce the vocabulary listed previously. The words can be introduced even if they are not in the specific reading you have chosen.

## GUIDED PRACTICE

Have students preview any headings and subheadings in the reading they have been asked to do. Have students read the selections.

**Read and Discuss:** Have students reread each section of the text and discuss the following:

- Why did Britain need the colonies to handle some of the financial burden of the Seven Years' War?
- Why did colonists feel the British Parliament should not tax them?
- Would the colonial reaction to the Sugar Act been different if the language of the act did not talk about taxes and if the economy had not been in a downturn?
- Why could the Currency Act, while not a tax act, affect the economy in the colonies much like a tax?
- Why can the Quartering Act be described as an indirect tax?
- Why could the Stamp Act, if it had been enforceable, have a large impact on colonists?
- How were the Townsend Acts and the Boston Massacre related?
- Why is the Tea Act, not a tax act itself, included in the acts surrounding the issue of no taxation without representation?

## MODEL

Assign students to five small groups. Give each group one act to consider. Have the students review the game board to discover the colonies as they were at the start of the Revolutionary War and review source materials. Each group should then develop a PowerPoint presentation on why its act might have impacted different colonies differently.

## INDEPENDENT PRACTICE

Remind students of the vocabulary introduced for their reading and ask them to attempt to include that vocabulary in appropriate ways in the writing activities they do.

### Writing Activities

**Narrative:** You are a newspaper publisher and have just heard about the Stamp Act. Write a letter to a family member telling him or her about the act, how you feel about it, and how it will impact your business if enforced.

**Inform or Explain:** Choose one of following acts and write an essay describing its intent, its implementation, and its true impact on the colonies:

- The Sugar Act, 1764
- The Quartering Act, 1765
- The Stamp Act, 1765
- The Townshend Acts, 1767
- The Tea Act, 1773

**Express an Opinion:** Benjamin Franklin testified before the House of Commons that a major complaint in the colonies was the imposition of internal taxes as opposed to external taxes. Does this fit into the argument of no taxation without representation? Were the colonists' concerns valid? Support your position using evidence from the readings.

## SHARING/REFLECTION

Have individuals or groups share and discuss their work with the class. Having groups present the information from their presentation developed in the previous model section can allow jigsaw learning where groups each add some information to class understanding. Also consider having students defend their opinion writing in front of the class as Franklin had to defend the colonies in front of the House of Commons.

## ASSESSMENT

Collect completed formative assessment (activity for Model section) and writing activities and review. Additional assessment will come from student presentations in front of the class defending their opinions. This is a chance to assess both the student as a speaker and the class as listeners. Student writing should demonstrate clear understanding of internal vs. external taxes.

## EXTENSION ACTIVITIES

**Further Research:** Find sources on the economy in Britain after the Seven Years' War to determine why it can be said that Britain won the war, but at great cost.

**Important Details:** Have students identify ten important details to know and justify their choices of those details using the Important Details sheet in the appendix and available online at www.teachingthroughgames.com for printing. Answers will vary.

**Develop a Timeline:** Place each of the acts appropriately on a timeline showing when it was passed and ended. Illustrate each act with a picture you draw or from the Internet that you feel represents the act.

## EXCERPTS FROM "THE EXAMINATION OF DOCTOR FRANKLIN, BEFORE AN AUGUST ASSEMBLY, RELATING TO THE REPEAL OF THE STAMP-ACT, &C"

Published in 1766

Q. What is your name, and place of abode?

A. Franklin, of Philadelphia.

**Q. Do the Americans pay any considerable taxes among themselves?**

**A. Certainly many, and very heavy taxes.**

Q. What are the present taxes in Pennsylvania, laid by the laws of the Colony?

A. There are taxes on all estates real and personal; a poll-tax; a tax on all offices, professions, trades and businesses, according to their profits; an excise on all wine, rum and other spirit; and a duty of ten pounds per head on all Negroes imported, with some other duties.

Q. For what purposes are those taxes laid?

A. For the support of the civil and

military establishment of the country, and to <u>discharge</u> the heavy debt contracted in the last war...

Q. Are not the Colonies, from their circumstances, very able to pay the stamp-duty?

A. In my opinion there is not gold and silver enough in the Colonies to pay the stamp duty for one year.

Q. Don't you know that the money arising from the stamps was all to be laid out in America?

A. I know it is appropriated by the act to the American Service; but it will be spent in the conquered Colonies, where the soldiers are, not in the Colonies that pay it...

Q. Do you think it right America should be protected by this country, and pay no part of the expense?

A. That is not the case. The colonies raised, clothed, and paid, during the last war, near 25,000 men, and spent many millions.

Q. Were you not reimbursed by Parliament?

A. We were <u>reimbursed</u> what, in your opinion, we had advanced beyond our proportion, or beyond what might reasonably be expected from us; and it was a very small part of what we spent. Pennsylvania, in particular, disbursed about 500,000 pounds, and the reimbursements, in the whole, did not exceed 60,000 pounds...

Q. Do not you think the people of America would submit to pay the stamp duty, if it was <u>moderated</u>?

A. No, never, unless compelled by force of arms...

Q. **What was the temper of America towards Great Britain before the year 1763?**

A. **The best in the world. They submitted willingly to the government of the Crown, and paid, in all their courts, obedience to acts of Parliament. Numerous as the people are in the several old provinces, they cost you nothing in forts, citadels, garrisons or armies, to keep them in <u>subjection</u>. They were governed by this country at the expense only of a little pen, ink and paper. They were led by a thread. They had not only a respect, but an affection, for Great Britain, for its laws, its customs and manners, and even a fondness for its fashions, that greatly increased the commerce. Natives of Britain were always treated with particular regard; to be an Old England-man, was, of itself, a character of some respect, and gave a kind of rank among us.**

Q. And what is their temper now?

A. Oh, very much altered.

Q. Did you ever hear the authority of Parliament to make laws for America questioned till lately?

A. The authority of Parliament was

allowed to be valid in all laws, except such as should lay internal taxes. It was never disputed in laying duties to regulate commerce...

**Q. In what light did the people of America use to consider the Parliament of Great Britain?**

**A. They considered the parliament as the great <u>bulwark</u> & security of their liberties and privileges, and always spoke of it with the utmost respect and veneration: arbitrary ministers, they thought, might possibly, at times, attempt to oppress them, but they relied on it, that the Parliament, on application, would always give <u>redress</u>. They remembered, with gratitude, a strong instance of this, when a bill was brought into Parliament with the clause to make royal instructions laws in the Colonies, which the House of Commons would not pass, and it was thrown out.**

**Q. And have they not still the same respect for Parliament?**

**A. No; it is greatly lessened.**

Q. To what cause is that owing?

**A. To a <u>concurrence</u> of causes; the restraints lately laid on their trade, by which the bringing of foreign gold and silver into the colonies was prevented; the prohibition of making paper money among themselves; and then demanding a new and heavy tax by stamps; taking away at the same time, trials by juries, and refusing to receive & hear their humble petitions.**

Q. Don't you think they would submit to the stamp-act, if it was modified, the obnoxious parts taken out, and the duties reduced to some particulars, of small moment.

A. No; they will never submit to it...

Q. What is your opinion of a future tax, imposed on the same principle with that of the Stamp Act? How would Americans receive it?

A. Just as they do this. They would not pay it.

Q. Have not you heard of the resolutions of this House, and of the House of Lords, asserting the right of Parliament relating to America, including a power to tax the people there?

A. Yes, I have heard of such resolutions.

Q. What will be the opinion of the Americans on those resolutions?

A. They will think them unconstitutional and unjust.

Q. Was it an opinion in America before 1763 that the Parliament had no right to lay taxes and duties there?

A. I have never heard any objection to the right of laying duties to regulate commerce; but a right to lay internal taxes was never supposed to be in Parliament, as we are not represented there.

Q. On what do you found your opinion,

that the people in America made any such distinction?

A. I know that whenever the subject has occurred in conversation where I have been present, it has appeared to be the opinion of every one, that we could not be taxed in a Parliament where we were not represented. But the payment of duties laid by act of Parliament, as regulations of commerce was never disputed...

Q. You say the Colonies have always submitted to <u>external taxes</u>, and object to the right of parliament only in laying <u>internal taxes</u>; now can you show that there is any kind of difference between the two taxes to the Colony on which they may be laid?

A. I think the difference is very great. An external tax is a duty laid on commodities imported; that duty is added to the first cost, and other charges on the <u>commodity</u>, and when it is offered to sale, makes a part of the price. If the people do not like it at that price, they refuse it; they are not obliged to pay it. But an internal tax is forced from the people without their consent, if not laid by their own representatives. The stamp-act says, we shall have no commerce, make no exchange of property with each other, neither purchase nor grant, nor recover debts; we shall neither marry, nor make our wills, unless we

pay such & such sums; and thus it is intended to extort our money from us, or ruin us by the consequences of refusing to pay it.

Q. But supposing the external tax or duty to be laid on the necessaries of life imported into your Colony, will not that be the same thing in its effects as an internal tax?

A. I know not a single article imported into the northern Colonies, but what they can either do without, or make themselves...

Q. Considering the resolutions of Parliament, as to the right, do you think, if the stamp-act is repealed, that the North Americans will be satisfied?

A. I believe they will.

Q. Why do you think so?

A. I think the resolutions of right will give them very little concern, if they are never attempted to be carried into practice. The Colonies will probably consider themselves in the same situation, in that respect, with Ireland; they know you claim the same right with regard to Ireland, but you never exercise it. And they may believe you never will exercise it in the Colonies, any more than in Ireland, unless on some very extraordinary occasion.

Q. But who are to be judges of that extraordinary occasion? Is it not the Parliament?

A. Though the Parliament may judge of

the occasion, the people, will think it can never exercise such a right, till representatives from the Colonies are admitted into Parliament, & that whenever the occasion arises, representatives will be ordered...

Q. Did the Americans ever dispute the controlling power of Parliament to regulate the commerce?

A. No.

**Q. Can anything less than a military force carry the Stamp Act into execution?**

**A. I do not see how a military force can be applied for that purpose.**

**Q. Why may it not?**

**A. Suppose a military force sent into America; they will find nobody in arms; what are they then to do? They cannot force a man to take stamps who chooses to do without them. They will not find a rebellion; they may indeed make one.**

Q. If the act is not repealed, what do you think will be the consequences?

A. A total loss of the respect and affection the people of America bear to this country, and of all the commerce that depends on that respect and affection.

Q. How can the commerce be affected?

A. You will find that, if the act is not repealed, they will take very little of your manufactures in a short time.

Q. Is it in their power to do without them?

A. I think they may very well do without them.

Q. Is it their interest not to take them?

A. The goods they take from Britain are either **necessaries**, mere **conveniences**, or **superfluities**. The first, as cloth, etc., with a little industry they can make at home; the second they can do without till they are able to provide them among themselves; and the last, which are much the greatest part, they can strike off immediately. They are mere articles of fashion, purchased and consumed because the fashion in a respected country; but will now be detested and rejected. The people have already struck off, by general agreement, the use of all goods fashionable in mournings, and many thousand pounds worth are sent back as unsaleable.

Q. Is it in their interest to make cloth at home?

A. I think they may at present get it cheaper from Britain, I mean of the same fineness and neatness of workmanship; but when one considers other circumstances, the restraints on their trade, and the difficulty of making **remittances**, it is their interest to make every thing.

Q. Suppose an act of internal regulations, connected with a tax, how would they receive it?

A. I think it would be objected to.

**Q. Then no regulation with a tax**

would be submitted to?

A. Their opinion is, that when aids to the Crown are wanted, they are to be asked of the several assemblies, according to the old established usage, who will, as they always have done, grant them freely. And that their money ought not to be given away without their consent, by persons at a distance, un-acquainted with their circumstances & abilities. The granting aids to the Crown, is the only means they have of recommending themselves to their sovereign, and they think it extremely hard and unjust, that a body of men, in which they have no representative should make a merit of itself of giving and granting what is not its own, but theirs, and deprive them of a right they esteem of the utmost value and importance, as it is the security of all their other rights...

Q. If the stamp-act should be repealed, would not the Americans think they could oblige Parliament to repeal every external tax law now in force.

A. It is hard to answer questions of what people at such a distance will think.

Q. But what do you imagine they will think were the motives of repealing the act?

A. I suppose they will think it was repealed from a conviction of its inexpediency; and they will rely upon it, that

while the same inexpediency subsists, you will never attempt to make such another.

Q. What do you mean by inexpediency?

A. I mean its inexpediency on several accounts; the poverty & inability of those who were to pay the tax; the general discontent it has occasioned, & the impracticability of enforcing it.

Q. If the act should be repealed, and the legislature should show its resentment to the opposers of the stamp-act, would the Colonies acquiesce in the authority of the legislature? What is your opinion they would do?

A. I don't doubt at all, that if the legislature repeal the stamp-act, the Colonies will acquiesce in the authority.

Q. But if the legislature should think fit to ascertain its right to lay taxes, by an act laying a small tax, contrary to their opinion, would they submit to pay the tax?

A. The proceedings of the people in America have been considered too much together. The proceedings of the assemblies have been very different from those of the mobs, & should be distinguished, as having no connection with each other. The assemblies have only peaceably resolved what they take to be their rights; they have taken no measures for opposition by force; they have not built a fort, raised a man, or provided a grain of ammunition, in order to such opposition. **The ringleaders of riots they think ought to be punished; they would punish them themselves, if they could. Every sober sensible man would wish to see rioters punished, as otherwise peaceable people have no security of person or estate.** But as to any internal tax, how small forever, laid by the legislature here on the people there, while they have no representatives in this legislature, I think it will never be submitted to. They will oppose it to the last. They do not consider it as at all necessary for you to raise money on them by your taxes, because they are, & always have been, ready to raise money by taxes among themselves, and to grant large sums, equal to their abilities, upon requisition from the Crown. They have not only granted equal to their abilities, but, during all the last war, they have granted far beyond their abilities, and beyond their proportion with this country, you yourselves being judges, to the amount of many hundred thousand pounds, and this they did freely and readily, only on a sort of promise from the secretary of state, that it should be recommended to Parliament to make them compensation. It was accordingly recommended to Parliament, in the most honorable manner, for them. America has been greatly misrepresented and abused here,

in papers, and pamphlets, and speeches, as ungrateful, and unreasonable, and unjust, in having put this nation to immense expense for their defense, and refusing to bear any part of that expense. The Colonies raised, paid and clothed, near 25,000 men during the last war, a number equal to those sent from Britain, and far beyond their proportion; they went deeply in debt in doing this, and all their taxes and estates are mortgages, for many years to come, for discharging that debt. Government here was at that time sensible of this. The Colonies were recommended to Parliament. **Every year the King sent down to the House a written message to this purpose. That his Majesty, being highly sensible of the zeal and vigor with which his faithful subjects in North America had exerted themselves, in defense of his Majesty's just rights and possession, recommended it to the House to take the same into consideration, and enable him to give them a proper compensation. You will find those messages on your own journals every year of the war to the very last, and you did accordingly give 200,000 Pounds annually to the Crown, to be distributed in such compensation to the Colonies. This is the strongest of all proofs that the Colonies, far from being unwilling to bear a share of the burden then, did exceed their** proportion, for if they had done less, or had only equaled their proportion, there would have been no room or reason for compensation. Indeed the sums reimbursed them, were by no means adequate to the expense they incurred beyond their proportion; but they never murmured at that; they esteemed their Sovereign's <u>approbation</u> of their zeal and fidelity, the approbation of this House, far beyond any other kind of compensation; therefore, there was no occasion for this act, to force money from a willing people, they had not refused giving money for the purposes of the act: no requisition had been made; they were always willing and ready to do what could reasonably be expected from them, and in this light they wish to be considered...

Q. If the Stamp Act should be repealed, would it induce the assemblies of America to acknowledge the right of Parliament to tax them, and would they erase their resolutions?

A. No, never.

Q. Is there no means of obliging them to erase those resolutions?

A. None that I know of; they will never do it, unless compelled by force of arms.

Q. Is there a power on earth that can force them to erase them?

A. No power, how great so ever, can force men to change their opinions...

Q. What used to be the pride of the Americans?

A. To indulge in the fashions and manufactures of Great Britain.

Q. What is now their pride?

A. To wear their old clothes over again, till they can make new ones.

# LESSON 3:
# RISING HOSTILITIES:

The American colonies continued to expand and were seen by the British to be important in fostering the well being of Britain. However, some colonists began to organize around the belief that Britain was not really respecting the citizens of the colonies as true British citizens. Complaints and protests slowly turned violent as mobs began to organize in opposition to British rule.

## HISTORICAL INFORMATION

### PROTESTS TURN VIOLENT

The Sons of Liberty was a very loosely organized underground group of individuals who were opposed to actions being taken by Britain. Its major concern was represented in the motto, "No Taxation Without Representation." The leaders—including notable figures such as John Adams, Samuel Adams, Benedict Arnold, John Hancock, Patrick Henry, and Paul Revere—were generally from the middle class, but they sought to involve the larger lower class through meetings and publications. The Sons of Liberty was founded in Boston in 1765; within a year, there were active chapters in all the colonies. The group served as a conduit for information on resistance to new acts. Their public meetings were often violent—barely controlled mobs roused by fiery speeches destroyed property and attacked British supporters or workers in colonial governments like tax collectors.

The Boston Massacre, in March 1770, was an incident that began when a small mob harassed a British sentinel and ended when a much larger mob with no weapons faced British soldiers with weapons. The mob was intent on having the soldiers fire on them, yelling at the soldiers to "fire." When one soldier was knocked down by a thrown object, he finally broke down and fired on the mob. Other soldiers fired without being given an order to do so, and in the end eleven men were hit, with five dying then or in the next few days. All but two of the soldiers, who witnesses said fired directly into the mob, were acquitted and all the colonists who were accused were acquitted. It is important to note that John Adams, a lawyer and member of the Sons of Liberty, defended the British soldiers. In his statements to the jury, Adams spoke sharply against the violence of the mob stating that the soldiers had a legal right to defend themselves and others against the mob. The statements made by Adams about mob violence in the trial, however, differed sharply from the statements of the Sons of Liberty as it encouraged new acts of violence.

The Gaspee Affair, in June 1772, was one violent action of the Sons of Liberty. Members of the Sons of Liberty were incensed over the actions of Lieutenant William Duddington, commander of the ship *Gaspee*. He was enforcing the custom laws without recognition of the rights of shippers and with no recourse for colonial merchants who were losing money when goods were taken. The Sons of Liberty group tricked the *Gaspee* into chasing another boat so that the larger British ship ran aground. It was then boarded by colonials; Duddington was wounded, the crew abandoned on shore, the bounty looted, and the ship burned

The Boston Tea Party, in November 1773, was another action, and possibly the most famous one, of the Sons of Liberty. Governor Hutchinson of Massachusetts called for a hard line against the protests over the Tea Act. He ordered that three ships in Boston Harbor remain despite colonists preventing the ships from unloading their cargos of tea. A group of colonists, some disguised as Mohawks, dumped all the tea chests from three vessels into Boston Harbor. John Adams argued that the incident was not a mob action but, rather, a protest action by people defending their right under British law for no taxation without representation. Retaliation by the British led to closing the port of Boston and creating new laws called the Coercive Acts. Looking back, the Boston Tea Party was a very important incident leading to the Revolutionary War. Not only was it a very notable direct action, but also the harsh response from Britain is what finally swayed popular opinion toward independence.

## THE INTOLERABLE ACTS

The Intolerable Acts, referred to as the Coercive Acts in Britain, was the name given by colonists to a series of actions by the British Parliament to punish Massachusetts after the Boston Tea Party. The first three acts directly targeted Massachusetts. The Boston Port Act demanded the closing of the port of Boston until full repayment was made to the British East India Company for the tea destroyed in the Boston Tea Party. Next, the Massachusetts Government Act sought to take all power from the colonials in government by requiring all appointments to be made by the royal governor, Parliament, or the king. Finally, the Administration of Justice Act allowed the royal governor to move trials for British officers accused of crimes to Britain if he felt they could not receive a fair trial in Massachusetts. This meant that any colonist accusing a British officer of a crime and needing to testify would have to pay for passage to Britain in order to press the charges. Though witnesses would be later reimbursed for the cost of travel, most colonists couldn't afford the initial cost and certainly couldn't afford to lose months of wages for the extended travel time.

The Quartering Act of 1774 affected all the colonies, not just Massachusetts. It required less of the colonists than the earlier Quartering Act because it did not require provision of the troops; however, it did allow for placing troops in unoccupied buildings. Though this act might have been ignored a few years earlier, in the heightened tensions of 1774, it was additional fuel for the anger of some colonists.

## THE FIRST CONTINENTAL CONGRESS

The First Continental Congress, held in September 1774, was the colonial response to the Intolerable Acts. All of the colonies, expect Georgia, were represented at the meeting. The Congress wanted to find a peaceful resolution to the growing problems with Britain and was still focused on seeking relief from taxation without representation; seeking independence was not yet even being considered. The Congress issued—with approval by all of the colonial governments except for Georgia and New York—a declaration of rights. The declaration reaffirmed the loyalty of the colonies to Britain, but called for Britain to recognize that they could not tax the colonies without the colonies having representation in Parliament. The Congress also passed the Articles of Association, calling for a boycott on British goods if the Intolerable Acts were not repealed and calling for reconvening if disputes were not resolved.

A Second Continental Congress was planned for May 10, 1775 to provide a deadline for British response, but that date would prove to be too late. After the outbreak of war in Massachusetts Colony on April 19, 1775, at the Battles of Lexington and Concord, when the Second Continental Congress did meet in May 1775, the delegates quickly realized that they needed to take on leadership of a larger effort for defense.

## LESSON PLAN

### ESSENTIAL QUESTION

What was the cause of escalating hostilities before the start of the Revolutionary War?

### VOCABULARY

The following vocabulary words are important concepts for this lesson on the rise of hostilities before the outbreak of the American Revolution.

- Hostilities
- Harass
- Recourse
- Retaliation

## SUGGESTED READING RESOURCES

### Primary Source Documents

"Case of Capt. Thomas Preston of the 29th Regiment." An account of the Boston Massacre by the captain leading the British troops involved written and sent to England from his jail cell in Boston.

*The Bloody Massacre Perpetrated in King Street, Boston on March 5th 1770 by a Party of the 29th Regiment.* This is an engraving by Paul Revere representing the scene from the Boston Massacre with an additional explanation in poetic form.

The original documents are both available online at http://www.masshist.org. These documents are included after the lesson in an annotated form. They are also available online at www.teaching throughgames.com for printing.

### Other Sources

Chapter 2: "The Continental Congress," which includes a document "The Association of the Continental Congress" in:

*The American Revolution and the Young Republic: 1763 to 1816*

Written by Britannica Educational Publishing

Published by Britannica Educational Publishing, 2011

ISBN: 9781615306688

## MINI READING LESSON

While you are reading the available text material or the suggested reading resources, attempt to answer the following questions: What events represented rising hostilities before the American Revolution? How was the same event reported and represented differently by both sides? Was war, as early as 1770, inevitable?

Introduce the previous vocabulary words. They can be introduced even if they are not in the specific reading you have chosen.

## GUIDED PRACTICE

Have students preview any headings and subheadings in the reading they have been asked to do. Have students read the selections.

### Read and Discuss

Have students reread each section of the text and discuss the following:

- What was the Sons of Liberty?
- What factors resulted in the Boston Massacre and how was the incident handled by both sides in the incident?
- Would the Boston Tea Party been such a decisive factor in the movement toward war if Britain had not taken the action it did?
- Did the First Continental Congress see themselves as launching a war against Britain? Why or why not?

### Model

Complete a brief description of each of the events listed on the worksheet titled "Rising Hostilities."

## INDEPENDENT PRACTICE

Remind students of the vocabulary introduced for their reading and ask them to attempt to include that vocabulary in appropriate ways in the writing activities they do.

### Writing Activities

**Narrative:** Take on the role of a colonist standing next to one of the people shot and killed at the Boston Massacre. Describe a YouTube video that might have appeared if such technology had existed at that time. Tell some of the words you might have used and describe the scenes.

**Inform or Explain:** Explain the focus of the First Continental Congress.

**Express an Opinion:** Was the Boston Tea Party justified? Why or why not?

## SHARING/REFLECTION

Have individuals or groups share and discuss their work with the class.

## ASSESSMENT

Collect completed formative assessment (activity for Model section) and writing activities and review. The rising hostilities sheet should include details on events including the Boston Tea Party and the Boston Massacre as well as information on the Sons of Liberty.

## EXTENSION ACTIVITIES

**Further Research:** Complete additional research on one of the following events: the Boston Massacre, the Gaspee Affair, or the Boston Tea Party. Develop a PowerPoint presentation or write an essay to present your findings. Be sure to include information on the colonial view and the British view.

**Important Details:** Have students identify ten important details to know and justify their choices of those details using Important Details sheet in the appendix and available online at www.teachingthroughgames.com for printing. Answers will vary.

**Develop a Timeline:** Place each of the events in the increase in hostilities appropriately on a timeline. Illustrate each act with a picture you draw or from the Internet that you feel represents the event as either historically correct or showing a bias. Indicate if you feel the picture is historically correct or biased.

# "CASE OF CAPT. THOMAS PRESTON OF THE 29TH REGIMENT"

IT is Matter of too great Notoriety to need any Proofs, that the Arrival of his Majesty's Troops in Boston was extremely obnoxious to it's Inhabitants. They have ever used all Means in their Power to weaken the Regiments, and to bring them into Contempt, by promoting and aiding Desertions, and with <u>Impunity</u>, even where there has been the clearest Evidence of the Fact, and by grossly and falsely <u>propagating</u> Untruths concerning them. On the Arrival of the 64th & 65th, their Ardour seemingly began to abate; it being too expensive to buy off so many; and Attempts of that Kind rendered too dangerous from the Numbers. -- But the same Spirit revived immediately on it's being known that those Regiments were ordered for Halifax, and hath ever since their Departure been breaking out with greater Violence. After their <u>Embarkation</u>, one of their Justices, not thoroughly acquainted with the People and their Intentions, on the Trial of the 14th Regiment, openly and publicly, in the Hearing of great Numbers of People, and from the Seat of Justice, declared, 'that the Soldiers must now take Care of themselves, nor trust too much to their Arms, for they were but a Handful; that the Inhabitants carried Weapons concealed under their Cloaths, and would destroy them in a Moment if they pleased.' This, considering the malicious Temper of the People, was an alarming Circumstance to the Soldiery. Since which several Disputes have happened between the Towns-People and Soldiers of both Regiments and the former being encouraged thereto by the <u>Countenance</u> of even some of the Magistrates, and by the Protection of all the Party against Government. In general such Disputes have been kept too secret from the Officers. **On the 2d instant, two of the 29th going through one Gray's Rope-Walk, the Ropemakers insultingly asked them if they would empty a Vault. This unfortunately had the desired Effect by provoking the Soldiers, and from Words they went to Blows. Both Parties suffered in this Affray, and finally, the Soldiers retired to their Quarters. The Officers, on the first Knowledge of this Transaction, took every Precaution in their Power to prevent any ill Consequences. Notwithstanding which, single Quarrels could not be prevented; the Inhabitants constantly provoking** and abusing the Soldiery. The Insolence, as well as utter Hatred of the Inhabitants to the Troops, increased daily; insomuch, that Monday and Tuesday, the 5th and 6th instant, were privately agreed on for a general Engagement; in consequence of which several of the Militia came from the Country, armed to join their Friends, menacing to destroy any who should oppose them. This Plan has since been discovered.

On Monday Night about Eight o'Clock two Soldiers were attacked and beat. But the Party of the Towns-People, in order to carry Matters to the utmost Length, broke into two Meeting-Houses, and rang the Alarm Bells, which I supposed was for Fire as usual, but was soon undeceived. About Nine some of the Guard came to and informed me, the Town-Inhabitants were assembling to attack the Troops, and that the Bells were ringing as the Signal for that Purpose, and not for Fire, and the Beacon intended to be fired to bring in the distant People of the Country. **This, as I was Captain of the Day, occasioned my repairing immediately to the Main-Guard. In my Way there I saw the People in great Commotion, and heard them use the most cruel and horrid Threats against the Troops. In a few Minutes after I reached the Guard, about an hundred** People passed it, and went towards **the Custom-House, where the King's Money is lodged. They immediately surrounded the Sentinel posted there, and with Clubs and other Weapons threatened to execute their Vengeance on him. I was soon informed by a Townsman, their Intention was to carry off the Soldier from his Post, and probably murder him.** On which I desired him to return for further Intelligence; and he soon came back and assured me he heard the Mob declare they would murder him. This I feared might be a Prelude to their plundering the King's Chest. **I immediately sent a non-commissioned Officer and twelve Men to protect both the Sentinel and the King's-Money, and very soon followed myself, to prevent (if possible) all Disorder; fearing lest the Officer and Soldiery by the Insults and Provocations of the Rioters, should be thrown off their Guard and commit some rash Act.** They soon rushed through the People, and, by charging their Bayonets in half Circle, kept them at a little Distance. Nay, so far was I from intending the Death of any Person, that I suffered the Troops to go to the Spot where the unhappy Affair took Place, without any Loading in their Pieces, nor did I ever give Orders for loading them. This remiss Conduct in me perhaps merits Censure; yet it is Evidence, resulting from the Nature of Things, which is the best and surest that can be offered, that my Intention was not to act offensively, but the contrary Part, and that not without Compulsion. The Mob still increased, and were more outrageous, striking their Clubs or Bludgeons one against another, and calling out, 'come on, you Rascals, you bloody Backs you Lobster Scoundrels; fire if you dare, G-d damn you, fire and be damn'd; we know you dare not;' and much more such Language was used. At this Time I was between the Soldiers and the Mob, parleying with and endeavoring all in my Power to persuade them to retire peaceably; but to no Purpose. They advanced to the Points of the Bayonets, struck some of them, and even the Muzzles of the Pieces, and seemed to be endeavoring to close with the Soldiers. On which some well-behaved Persons asked me if the Guns were charged: I replied, yes. They then asked me if I intended to order the Men to fire; I answered no, by no Means; observing to them, that I was advanced before the Muzzles of the Men's Pieces, and must fall a Sacrifice if they fired; that the Soldiers were upon the Half-cock and charged Bayonets, and my giving the word fire, under those Circumstances, would prove me no Officer. While I was thus speaking, one of the Soldiers, having received a severe Blow with a Stick, stept a little on one Side, and instantly fired, on which turning to and asking him why he fired without Orders, I was struck with a Club on my Arm, which for sometime deprived my of the Use of it; which Blow, had it been placed on my Head, most probably would have destroyed me. On this general Attack was made on the Men by a great Number of heavy Clubs, and Snow-Balls being thrown at them, by which all our Lives were in imminent Danger; some Persons at the same Time from behind calling out, 'Damn your Bloods, why don't you fire? Instantly three or four of the Soldiers fired, one after another, and directly after three more in the same Confusion and Hurry.

The Mob then ran away, except three unhappy Men who instantly expired, in which Number was Mr. Gray, at whose Rope-Walk the prior Quarrel took Place; one more in since dead, three others are dangerously, and four slightly wounded. The Whole of this melancholy Affair was transacted in almost 20 Minutes. On my asking the Soldiers why they fired without Orders, they said they heard the Word "Fire," and supposed it came from me. This might be the Case, as many of the Mob called out "Fire, fire," but I assured the Men that I gave no such Order, that my Words were, "Don't fire, stop your Firing:" In short it was scarce possible for the Soldiers to know who said fire, or don't fire, or stop your Firing. On the People's assembling again to take away the dead Bodies, the Soldiers, supposing them coming to attack them, were making ready to fire again, which I prevented by striking up their Firelocks with my Hand. Immediately after a Townsman came and told me, that 4 or 5000 People were assembled in the next Street, and had sworn to take my Life with every Man's with me; on which I judged it unsafe to remain there any longer, and therefore sent the Party and Sentry to the Main-Guard, where the street is narrow and short, there telling them off into Street Firings, divided and planted them at each End of the Street to secure their Rear, momently expecting an Attack, as there was a constant Cry of the Inhabitants, "To Arms, to Arms, – turn out with your Guns," and the Town Drums beating to Arms. I ordered my Drum to beat to Arms, and being soon after joined by the different Companies of the 29th Regiment, I formed them as the Guard into Street Firings. The 14th Regiment also got under Arms, but remained at their Barracks. I immediately sent a Serjeant [Sergeant] with a Party to Col. Dalrymple,

the Commanding Officer, to acquaint him with every Particular. Several Officers going to join their Regiment were knocked down by the Mob, one very much wounded, and his Sword taken from him. The Lieutenant Governor and Col. Carr soon after met at the Head of the 29th Regiment, and agreed that the Regiment should retire to their Barracks, and the People to their Houses; but I kept the Piquet to strengthen the Guard. It was with great Diffculty that the Lieutenant Governor prevailed on the People to be quiet and retire: At last they all went off excepting about an Hundred.

**A Council was immediately called, on the breaking up of which three Justices met, and issued a Warrant to apprehend me and eight Soldiers. On hearing of this Procedure, I instantly went to the Sheriff and surrendered myself, though for the Space of four Hours I had it in my Power to have made my Escape, which I most undoubtedly should have attempted, and could have easily executed, had I been the least conscious of any Guilt.**

On the Examination before the Justices, **two Witnesses swore that I gave the Men Orders to fire; the one testified he was within two Feet of me; the other, that I swore at the Men for not firing at the first Word. Others swore they heard me use the Word "Fire," but whether do or do not fire** they could not say; others, that they heard the Word "Fire," but could not say if it came from me. The next Day they got five or six more to swear I gave the Word to fire. So bitter and inveterate are many of the Malcontents here, that they are industriously using every Method to fish out Evidence to prove it was a concerted Scheme to murder the Inhabitants. Others are infusing the utmost Malice and Revenge into the Minds of the People who are to be my Jurors by false Publications, Votes of Towns, and all other Artifices, that so from a settled Rancour against the Officers and Troops in general, the Suddenness of my Trial after the Affair, while the People's Minds are all greatly inflamed, I am though perfectly innocent, under most unhappy Circumstances, having nothing in Reason to expect but the Loss of Life in a very ignominious Manner, without the Interposition of his Majesty's Royal Goodness.

Boston-Gaol, Monday, 12th March 1770. Messieurs EDES & GILL,

PERMIT me thro' the Channel of your Paper, to return my Thanks in the most publick Manner to the Inhabitants in general of this Town -- who throwing aside all Party and Prejudice, have with the utmost Harmony and Freedom stept forth Advocates for Truth, in Defence of my injured Innocence, in the late unhappy Affair that happened on Monday Night last: And to assure them, that I shall ever have the highest Sense of the Justice they have done me,

Which will be ever gratefully remembered, by Their much obliged and most obedient humble Servant,

THOMAS PRESTON.

## ENGRAVING OF THE BOSTON MASSACRE BY PAUL REVERE

Unhappy Boston! see thy Sons deplore,
Thy hallow'd Walks besmear'd with guiltless Gore:
While faithless P--n and his savage Bands,
With murd'rous Rancour stretch their bloody HANDS;
Like fierce Barbarians grinning o'er their Prey,
Approve the Carnage and enjoy the Day.
If scalding drops from Rage from Anguish Wrung
If speechless Sorrows lab'ring for a Tongue.
Or if a weeping World can ought appease
The plaintive Ghosts of Victims such as these;

A glorious Tribute which embalms the Dead.
But know, FATE Summons to that awful Goal.
Where JUSTICE strips the Murd'rer of his Soul:
Should Venal C -- ts the scandal of the Land,
Snatch the relentless Villain from her Hand,
Keen Execrations on this Plate inscrib'd,
Shall reach a JUDGE who never can be brib'd.

The unhappy Sufferers were Messs. SAML. GRAY SAML MAVERICK, JAMS CALDWELL, CRISPUS ATTUCKS & PATK CARR Killed. Six wounded; two of them (CHRISTR MONK & JOHN CLARK) Mortally

# LESSON 4:
# THE WAR BEFORE THE DECLARATION

The American Revolution actually began before the Declaration on Independence was signed. The first shots of the war were fired on April 19, 1775, in the Battles of Lexington and Concord in Massachusetts. When the Second Continental Congress met a month later, they quickly moved to form a Continental Army under the leadership of George Washington. The Continental Army went on the offensive, invading British held Canada before the Declaration of Independence was even presented or approved by the various independent colonies. Even after the publication of the Declaration, not everyone wanted independence. Many colonists remained loyal to Britain and took up arms as loyalist militia who fought alongside the British army against their fellow colonists.

## HISTORICAL INFORMATION

### THE SHOT HEARD 'ROUND THE WORLD

> By the rude bridge that arched the flood,
> Their flag to April's breeze unfurled,
> Here once the embattled farmers stood,
> And fired the shot heard round the world.
> —Ralph Waldo Emerson[9]

Writing his "Concord Hymn" in 1837, Ralph Waldo Emerson was able to look back to the first shots of the American Revolutionary War in 1775 and see the incredible impact the war had on the world. Britain lost the war, but as we will see, it ended up in a better financial position than the French who supported the colonists. Debt from France's involvement in the American Revolution led to the French Revolution starting in 1789. The rise of Napoleon Bonaparte from the chaos after the French Revolution would dramatically change Europe and the rest of the world. After the American and French Revolutions, monarchies and religious governments declined; the world turned toward more democratic forms of government. In April 1775, however, the colonial militias who gathered in Concord to resist the British army were not thinking about any of these issues. At the time, there wasn't even a general consensus that independence was what they were fighting for.

Following the Battles of Lexington and Concord, the emboldened colonial militias followed the British retreat and laid siege to the British forces in Boston. On June 17, 1775, in the Battle of Bunker Hill, British forces attacked colonial forces attempting to reinforce Bunker Hill and Breed's Hill. The colonial forces were trying to create positions from which they could fire artillery onto British forces in Boston. Though considered a British victory as the attack forced the colonials to retreat, the British army suffered much higher losses, including many officers. The colonial army had also demonstrated that they could stand up to the veteran forces of the British army in a regular battle, not just in the hit-and-run tactics of Lexington and Concord.

## THE SECOND CONTINENTAL CONGRESS

When the Second Continental Congress met on May 10, 1775, war had been raging in Massachusetts for almost a month. After debate, the Congress moved in June to formalize a larger resistance and formed the Continental Army as the official army of the united colonies under the command of George Washington. Washington had commanded troops in the French and Indian War. Despite these actions of war, the Congress was not yet considering it a war of independence. As it explained in a Declaration of Causes published on July 6, 1775, the war was a result of British aggression that had forced the colonies to choose between "an unconditional submission to the tyranny of irritated Ministers, or resistance by force."[10] The Second Continental Congress emphatically stated that it had "not raised armies with ambitious designs of separating from Great Britain, and establishing independent states" and wished to reassure readers that it did not mean to "dissolve that union which has so long and so happily subsisted between us, and which we sincerely wish to see restored."[11] In the last words of the Declaration of Causes from July of 1775, the conflict was clearly established as a "civil war" within the empire, not a colonial revolution.

Two days later, on July 8, 1775, the Second Continental Congress sent the Olive Branch Petition to King George asking for royal intervention to protect the colonies from Parliament. By the time the petition arrived in London at the end of August, however, it was too late. King George had heard of the British losses at Bunker Hill had already issued the Proclamation for Suppressing Rebellion and Sedition stating that the American colonies were in a state of rebellion and ordering the British army to crush the rebels. Radical colonial leaders used the rejection of the Olive Branch Petition as evidence that there was no possibility of a peaceful resolution to the conflict. As Patrick Henry famously stated in a 1775 speech to the Virginia House of Burgess asking that Virginia send troops to support Massachusetts and the Continental Army being organized by the Continental Congress, this was a matter of liberty or death.

## THE INVASION OF CANADA

Having organized the Continental Army under the command of General George Washington, the new American forces quickly went on the offensive against the British forces with a bold plan to free Canada. The British colony of Quebec—the name at the time for what we would now consider most of eastern Canada, not just the current Province of Quebec—had been won by Britain from France after the French and Indian War. The Continental Congress hoped that pushing the British out of Quebec would encourage them to join with the thirteen American colonies.

The path into Quebec was open following the capture of the strategically critical Fort Ticonderoga at the southern tip of Lake Champlain. Fort Ticonderoga was built to control the end of a long valley that, with the Adirondacks to the west and the White

Mountains to the east, was one of the only passable land routes north to Canada. Ethan Allen and his Green Mountain Boys militia captured the British fort with the help of Colonel Benedict Arnold. Arnold would later turn traitor, but then he was one of the top military leaders in the new American forces. Surprised in a dawn raid, the British forces surrendered the fort without a single shot being fired. Though the surprise attack was a brilliant tactical move, it must also be noted that this happened on May 10, 1775, the very date that the Second Continental Congress was convening and well before the outbreak of general hostilities.

General Richard Montgomery led the main attack north through the Champlain Valley into Canada starting in August 1775. By November, the Continental Army had reached Montreal and occupied it without much fight. Some of the Canadian colonists ended up joining with the Continental Army as it pushed toward Quebec City. Benedict Arnold was leading a second force toward Quebec City as well, taking an eastern route through modern-day Maine. Montgomery's and Arnold's forces, helped out by some of the French-Canadians who saw this as a chance for freedom from British rule, joined together in December to lay siege to Quebec City. On December 30, the Continental Army attacked, with disastrous results. General Montgomery was killed and Arnold injured along with thirty additional soldiers killed and over four hundred captured. Though Arnold bravely maintained the siege through the winter, when new leadership arrived in the spring of 1776 a retreat was ordered. Even though Bunker Hill had technically been a loss—the overwhelming number of British loses made it a very costly victory—the siege of Quebec City was the first true defeat of the Continental Army.

## Choosing Sides: Loyalists and Patriots in America

Even as war was breaking out all around them, not everyone in the thirteen colonies wanted to fight. About 20 percent of colonists calling themselves Loyalists remained devoted to the king. The Patriots, those who were increasingly calling for independence, typically referred to the Loyalists as Tories, naming them for a British political philosophy that granted more power to the king as opposed to Parliament. The Patriots were then also called Whigs, after another British political party.

Echoing the closing words of the Declaration of Causes that referred to the emerging war as a civil war within the British Empire, the American Revolution truly was the first American civil war. About 19,000 Loyalists joined the British army as regular troops. In comparison, the official Continental Army for the Patriot side at its largest had only about 17,000 soldiers. General Washington, enduring a tough winter at Valley Forge in 1777–1778, lamented about the "quantity of provisions that goes daily into Philadelphia" sent by Loyalists to support the British army.[12]

Even as the Continental Congress organized itself and the colonies, many Loyalists still saw the Patriots as the mobs that had instigated violent attacks upon those who tried to work with Britain in the previous decade. The Sons of Liberty had tarred and feathered many business and government leaders who tried to work with the British in the lead up to the revolution. Now those Loyalists took up arms to fight against the Patriots. In some battles, including the Battle of Kings Mountain fought in North Carolina in 1780, all of the soldiers were colonists. At Kings Mountain, the only non-American was the commander of the Loyalist militia, a British major, Patrick Ferguson. This battle is held up as an example of the violence of the civil war actions during the American Revolution. Even as the Loyalists tried to surrender after the death of Major Ferguson, the Patriot militia refused to accept the surrender and continued to kill the Loyalists. In the end, only 29 Patriots were killed, but 290 Loyalists were killed. Whether on the battlefield or in the cities where Patriot mobs continued to attack and kill suspected Loyalists, this was a vicious fight between neighbors.

## THE CAUSE OF AMERICA

By 1776, the Patriots were gaining more support throughout the colonies. The war had spread and King George's rejection of peace offerings suggested that there was no possibility of a resolution that kept the colonies as part of the British Empire. The calls for independence were beginning to be voiced more loudly and by more people. Thomas Paine expressed this opinion in *Common Sense*, one of the most famous revolutionary pamphlets published January 10, 1776. "Under our present denomination of British subjects," Paine argued, "we can neither be received nor heard abroad; the custom of all Courts is against us, and will be so, until by an independence we take rank with other nations."[13] Paine laid out in his pamphlet a call to action for the cause of America. "Let the names of Whig and Tory be extinct;" he wrote, "and let none other be head among us, than those of a good citizen, an open and resolute friend, and a virtuous supporter of the RIGHTS of MANKIND and of the FREE AND INDEPENDENT STATES OF AMERICA."[14] In this statement he echoed the famous political cartoon created by Benjamin Franklin in 1754, "Join, or Die," that represented the thirteen colonies as a snake cut into sections. By May of 1776, the Continental Congress was ready to move toward independence and passed a resolution calling on all of the colonies to form governments—replacing resistant governments as needed and ousting Loyalists—that would authorize independence. The delegates were ready to take a step unthinkable only a year earlier. The colonies were ready to declare independence from the British Empire.

## LESSON PLAN

### ESSENTIAL QUESTION

What are the many factors of war that can determine the outcome?

### VOCABULARY

The following vocabulary words are important concepts for this lesson about the American Revolution:

- British Regulars
- Loyalist militia

- Continental Army
- Patriot militia
- Tory
- Whig
- Truce
- Treason

## SUGGESTED READING RESOURCES

*The American Revolution and the Young Republic: 1763 to 1816*
Written by Britannica Educational Publishing
Published by Britannica Educational Publishing, 2011
ISBN: 9781615306688

## GAME LESSON

For this lesson, learners will play through the Siege of Quebec scenario for 1775: Rebellion. Introduce the game and game vocabulary. Use the game board as a focal point for introducing the game components to the students. The scenario setup and rules differ slightly from the regular game. In the Siege of Quebec, players will need to control cities by having their units in the region with the city. For each city controlled this way, the player will place a control flag on the city at the start of their turn. The game still ends with the playing of both truce cards for either side with victory points scored for city control flags. Note that Quebec City, the site of the siege and the target for the Continental Army, counts as two control flags.

The following concepts are important to understanding the game and mechanisms needed to play.

- Siege
- Surrender
- Rendezvous

- Reinforcements
- Sally

## GUIDED PRACTICE

Have students play the Seige of Quebec scenario following the setup and rules in the 1775 rulebook and then discuss. Looking at the game components and reviewing how the game is played and considering text material on the battles of the war at the start of hostilities, determine several factors that led to success in battles.

- What event is known as the shot that was heard "round the world" and why was that term given to the event?
- What happened at Lexington, Concord, Bunker Hill, Fort Ticonderoga, and the Seige of Quebec? Who were the winners and losers of these events?
- What arguments did the Patriots and Loyalists put forth to support their positons?
- What happened between the Loyalist and Patriot militias?

## MODEL

As a whole class, have the students explore the cards in the bags in GAME 1775: Rebellion that have white and yellow cubes to discover the concept of Loyalist and Patriot militia. Tell them to review all the cards including the pictures on the cards for some insights into facts about the militia and concepts that are related to the Loyalist and Patriot sides. Then have them work in small groups to summarize the findings of the class work and reach conclusions about Loyalists and Patriots.

## INDEPENDENT PRACTICE

Remind students of the vocabulary introduced for their reading and ask them to attempt to include that vocabulary in appropriate ways in the writing activities they do.

## Writing Activities

**Narrative:** Two colonists who have been long-term friends meet at the local general store. One is a Loyalist and one is for independence. Write a dialogue that might take place that develops the strong feelings of each and the reasons for those feelings. Let them part expressing regret for the end of their friendship.

**Inform or Explain:** Explain the myth of Paul Revere and how that myth relates to the reality of the events at Concord and Lexington.

**Express an Opinion:** If you had been alive at the time of the revolution, would you have been a Loyalist or a Patriot? Why?

## SHARING/REFLECTION

Have students or groups share and discuss their writing with the class. Ask students to reflect on how their perception of the American Revolution has changed based on what they learned about the war before the Declaration of Independence and the aspects of the revolution as a civil war between colonists.

## ASSESSMENT

Collect completed materials and writing activities and review them. Well-constructed responses for the sharing/reflection will demonstrate understanding of the Patriot invasion of Canada as happening before the Declaration of Independence. Students should also clearly write about the internal conflicts between Loyalists and Patriots.

## EXTENSION ACTIVITIES

**Further Research:** Research a recent war, possibly the wars in Vietnam, Iraq, or Afghanistan, to determine if a declaration of war preceded the actual war. Choose a way to share your findings and how you determined them.

**Important Details:** Have students identify ten important details to know about the war before the Declaration of Independence and justify their choices of those details using Important Details sheet in the appendix and available online at www.teachingthroughgames.com for printing. Answers will vary.

# LESSON 5:
# INDEPENDENCE DECLARED
# AND GAINED

After the Declaration of Independence was passed, the British moved to counter-attack against the aggression of the colonists. As the war continued, both sides sought help from other countries; after the Patriots stopped a major British advance at Saratoga, New York, France openly supported America. While a stalemate was reached in the northern colonies, the war in the southern colonies went differently. As the war went on, its popularity in Britain waned as it was hurting the economy. With the Treaty of Paris, both the British and the American colonies made gains and the colonies moved into the phase of forming a new country.

## HISTORICAL INFORMATION

### DECLARATION OF INDEPENDENCE

> *WHEN in the course of human Events, it becomes necessary for one People to dissolve the Political Bands which have connected them with another, and to assume among the Powers of the Earth, the separate and equal Station to which the Laws of Nature and of Nature's God entitle them, a decent Respect to the Opinions of Mankind requires that they should declare the causes which impel them to the Separation.*
> —The Declaration of Independence[15]

As colonial governments fell into line behind the idea of independence, their delegates to the Continental Congress were directed to support the process of separating from Britain. Thomas Jefferson, a representative from Virginia, was appointed to the committee drafting the statement for separation and ended up writing much of the Declaration of Independence. Jefferson's philosophies regarding government and society are strongly represented in the document, though a section he wrote criticizing slavery was removed. The

Declaration was the formal introduction to the world of a new country, the United States of America. It is critical to note, however, that in 1776 the United States were treated as a plural entity and a plural noun; today we use United States as a singular noun.

In 1776, the case for independence was laid out in the preamble of the Declaration. "That whenever any Form of Government becomes destructive of these ends," Jefferson wrote, "it is the Right of the People to alter or to abolish it, and to institute new Government..." [16] This action, he cautioned, was not to be taken except in the most dire of circumstances. "Governments long established should not be changed for light and transient causes...But when a long train of abuses and usurpations, pursuing invariably the same Object evinces a design to reduce them under absolute Despotism, it is their right, it is their duty, to throw off such Government..."[17] By the summer of 1776, the thirteen colonies felt that there was no possible response to the continuing actions of the British Parliament and King George other than to throw off that government.

Attempts at peaceful resolution in 1775 had failed. William Pitt, a prominent member of Parliament proposed three different solutions in February 1775 that were defeated in successive votes. The first was to grant the colonies self-government, the second was to withdraw troops from Boston to alleviate the immediate threat of war, and the final suggestion was to attempt conciliation through mutual concessions. Had any one of these passed, it might have de-escalated the situation. Instead, the Conciliatory Resolution that was passed was an appeal to each individual colony to provide resources to suppress the rebellion in other colonies. The Continental Congress rejected this, seeing it correctly as an attempt to divide and conquer. Parliament similarly rejected the Olive Branch Petition sent by the Continental Congress in July 1775, which asked for some minor concessions including free trade and taxation equal to that imposed on England.

Writing the Declaration a year later, Jefferson felt that diplomatic methods had been attempted to no success. As he wrote in the Declaration: "In every state of these Oppressions We have Petitioned for Redress in the most humble terms: Our repeated Petitions have been answered only by repeated injury."[18] The question, however, is why the Continental Congress waited so long to actually declare independence? The Declaration was issued more than a year after the war began at Lexington and Concord; a year after the Continental Congress had organized the Continental Army to fight the British. The initial invasion and siege of Quebec was undertaken before a formal declaration of independence. The answer is that the Declaration was as much a public relations event as a political statement. It was timed to celebrate George Washington's retaking of Boston in March 1776, and the general rejection of the last Loyalist governments and British forces.

## BRITISH COUNTER-ATTACK

After the Declaration of Independence, British forces moved quickly to counter-attack and regain control of the rebellious colonies. In late July 1776, the British army and navy under control of brothers General William Howe and Admiral Lord Richard Howe respectively, sailed from Halifax, Nova Scotia, to attack New York City. The armies met on Long Island in the Battle of Brooklyn. General Washington and the Continental Army were entrenched on Brooklyn Heights, but after General Howe landed on Staten Island, Washington moved his army to Manhattan to defend the city. General Howe—having a huge advantage with 32,000 troops to Washington's 10,000—split his forces and attacked the Continental Army on two sides. Washington was forced to give up the city and retreat back to his prepared defenses on Brooklyn Heights. Despite an overwhelming victory, General Howe did not press the attack and allowed Washington and the Continental Army to escape. Washington retreated into Pennsylvania, leaving the British to control New York City.

One possible reason for General Howe allowing Washington to escape was that he and his brother still believed that there could be a diplomatic resolution to the war. After the Battle of Brooklyn, Admiral Lord Richard Howe met with Benjamin Franklin, John Adams, and Edward Rutledge to talk about a possible truce. Howe's ability to negotiate had been severely limited by Parliament, but he was allowed to offer pardons and once again to suggest the terms of the Conciliatory Proposal. Franklin wrote the response from the Continental Congress rejecting Howe's offer stating that there was no need for pardons, as the colonies had done nothing wrong. In the rejection, Franklin also called out the British for "bringing foreign mercenaries to deluge our settlements with blood."[19] In this, Franklin was referring to the Hessian mercenaries hired by Britain from the German states to supplement the regular British army. In all, about 30,000 Hessians fought in the American Revolution including 18,000 at the Battle of Brooklyn.

## FOREIGN TROOPS AND THE WAR BY PROXY

Britain's use of Hessian mercenaries wasn't the only foreign involvement in the war. In many ways the American Revolution, like the French and Indian War before, was just another proxy war for the ongoing hostilities between Britain and France. The French and Indian War was the North American front for the Seven Years' War, and as hostilities arose again in North America France was quick to encourage the colonies. In early 1776, even before the Declaration of Independence had been passed, France was already supplying the Patriots with gunpowder and weapons. In December 1776, Benjamin Franklin was sent to France to serve as the new American ambassador and to encourage additional support.

France was unwilling to commit to a more formal recognition of America until the new country had proved itself capable of winning independence. After Washington's retreat from New York City, the Continental Army was pushed back through New Jersey to Pennsylvania. On December 25, 1776, General Washington crossed the Delaware River—an act memorialized in the famous painting on introduction of this book—to attack the primarily Hessian forces in Trenton, New Jersey. This decisive victory turned the tide; suddenly the retreat from New York City was ended and prospects looked good for Washington. Franklin used this victory to continue to pressure France for support.

In the following year, the war continued to go well for the colonies. Even though Philadelphia was lost to the British, a major British attack from Canada led by General John Burgoyne was stopped in Saratoga, New York, in October 1777. General Burgoyne was surrounded and forced to surrender as Patriot militias responded in great numbers. By the end of the battles the American army in Saratoga had grown from 9,000 to 15,000 troops, more than double the about 7,000 British soldiers. The incredible defeat of General Burgoyne's army—more than 6,200 soldiers surrendered with more than 1,000 more killed or wounded compared to Patriot losses of about 330 killed or wounded—showed France that the colonies might really be able to win.

In late 1777, Louis XVI, king of France, decided to formalize support for the new United States of America. In February 1778, the Treaty of Alliance formally recognized the new country and pledged military support. In response, Britain declared war on France in March 1778; there were a series of naval battles and engagements in the Caribbean. France's confirmation of the United States also led Spain to declare for the Americans in 1779. The Dutch Republic supported the colonies informally but did not want to become part of the war; despite this, Britain declared war on the Dutch Republic in 1780. One of the earliest, and most famous, instances of French involvement in the war effort were French aristocratic volunteers that travelled to America in 1777 to support Washington. The Marquis de Lafayette and Pierre Charles L'Enfant were with General Washington and the Continental Army in their winter quarters at Valley Forge in 1777–1778 and were instrumental in securing additional French support that would prove vital to American success. Also at Valley Forge was a Prussian aristocrat, Baron Friedrich Wilhelm von Steuben. Prussia, part of modern-day Germany, was at the time an independent kingdom fighting against other German states. Steuben, who had connections to France, travelled to America to serve as a drillmaster and later inspector general of the Continental Army. His training techniques and camp plans helped alleviate sickness that had plagued Valley Forge and better prepared the Continental Army for combat success in the coming years.

## Yorktown and the End of the War

As the war in the north stalled in 1778 with the Americans retaking Philadelphia but Britain holding strong in New York City, the action moved south. Many of the battles in the southern colonies were fought between foreign troops—Hessian mercenaries for the British and newly arrived French Regulars for the Americans—or between Patriot and Loyalists militias. In December 1778, the British captured Savannah, Georgia, and in 1780 they moved north to take Charleston, South Carolina, as well. The pressure from Patriot militias and French Regulars was too much, however, and the British forces led by General Charles Cornwallis started north toward Virginia. After a series of movements and battles, Cornwallis and the British army made their final stand in Yorktown, Virginia, in August 1781. The decision to base the British position on a peninsula jutting into the Chesapeake Bay may seem questionable, but Cornwallis was just expecting to hold out until the British navy could evacuate him.

Fortunately for America, the British navy did not arrive as expected. Instead a large French fleet from the Caribbean under the command of Admiral De Grasse arrived with additional troops and siege equipment to supplement Lafayette's land forces preventing Cornwallis from leaving Yorktown. Lafayette, the French aristocratic volunteer we first encountered at Valley Forge, was now one of Washington's most trusted commanders. Upon learning that Lafayette had Cornwallis pinned, Washington immediately began marching south. Washington and the main Continental Army forces had been preparing to attack New York City, now they were headed to Virginia. In early September, De Grasse's French Fleet defeated British reinforcements sent south from New York City in the Battle of the Chesapeake. The victory secured French control of the Chesapeake Bay—a long body of water the stretches north to Pennsylvania—and allowed French ships to meet Washington's army just south of Philadelphia to provide faster transport to Yorktown. Still expecting the promised reinforcements and evacuation,

Cornwallis remained in Yorktown even though the situation was growing dire.

In late September 1781, the combined armies of Washington and Lafayette, along with French navel support and marines, began the final siege of Yorktown. Seeing the futility of his situation, Cornwallis began negotiating terms of surrender on October 17. Washington used the surrender ceremony as a way to advance the political and diplomatic positions of the new United States. First, despite the British having snubbed the colonial forces in the 1780 surrender of Charleston by preventing them from marching to surrender under their colors—the battle and national flags of the army—Washington insisted that the British be granted this honor. Washington also allowed a single British ship to pass through the French naval blockade without any inspection. Though on paper this was done to allow Cornwallis to send a message to the British commanders in New York City, the real reason Washington agreed to this was that it allowed Loyalist militia to leave Yorktown before the surrender. This would have been done to prevent retaliation against Loyalists.

The surrender of Cornwallis's forces at Yorktown, a major portion of the British forces in America, was an incredible shock to the British. In December 1781, a resolution in the British Parliament calling for an end to the war was defeated by only one vote. Prime Minister North, however, was soon removed from office and even King George was considering abdicating the throne. Though minor skirmishes continued, the siege of Yorktown was the last major battle of the American Revolution. In March 1782, the new British commander was given orders to stop all offensive operations in preparation for treaty negotiations.

## THE TREATY OF PARIS AND AFTERMATH

In April 1782, peace negotiations were begun in Paris. Benjamin Franklin, John Adams, John Jay, and Henry Laurens represented America and fought strongly for major concessions from the British. In the end, the official Treaty of Paris was signed on September 3,

1783. In the treaty, Britain acknowledged the creation of the United States of America as a free country. The treaty also defined new boundaries for the United States and greatly increased the size of the new country. Loyalists who fled to Canada or Britain were supposed to be compensated for property that had been seized by the new states, but in actually most never received any restitution. The treaty was still a critical turning point for the new country as it established America as an instant power. The United States gained enormous amounts of land as compared to what was gained by their European allies, the French and Spanish.

Washington's diplomatic treatment of the British at Yorktown and the relatively fair treaty terms meant that diplomatic relations between Britain and America recovered relatively quickly. Britain's stunning loss, and the sensitive way that Washington handled it, made it easier for Britain to come to terms with the emergence of the former colonies as a new, independent country. Trade resumed easily with both sides still having contacts and established interests. By 1794, barely ten years after the end of the American Revolution, Britain and American negotiators met again in London to sign the Jay Treaty, which resolved some lingering border issues and averted a return to fighting. In return, the Americans granted Britain "most favored nation" trading status that simplified tariffs and trade rules and led to rapid economic growth for both countries during the late 1790s.

In contrast, France, still burdened by debts from the Seven Years' War, fell further into debt after helping the United States in the American Revolution. Even as British and American trade began to return to pre-war levels, France continued to falter. The result was the French Revolution, a period of prolonged fighting within France lasting from 1789 until 1799 when Napoleon Bonaparte seized control in a coup. Napoleon's rise to power and the Napoleonic Wars that followed as he sought to expand the French Empire in the early 1800s would once again thrust Europe and America into a new war. But that, as they say, is another story—and another game, 1812: The Invasion of Canada.

# LESSON PLAN

## Essential Question

Why might a revolution end in independence, and why might it not?

## Vocabulary

The following vocabulary words are important concepts for this lesson about the Declaration of Independence and the end of the American Revolution:

- Treaty
- War by proxy
- Surrender
- Marines
- Colors
- Blockade
- Most favored nation

## Suggested Reading Resources

### Primary Source Document

### "Alphabet for Little Masters and Misses"

This production appeared in a ballad sheet in the early part of 1775 and was afterward reprinted in the *Constitutional Gazette*, with a slight abridgment in the text.

A, stands for Americans, who scorn to be slaves;

B, for Boston, where fortitude their freedom saves;

C, stands for Congress, which, though loyal, will be free;

D, stands for defence, 'gainst force and tyranny.

Stand firmly, A and Z,

We swear for ever to be free!

E, stands for evils, which a civil war must bring;

F, stands for fate, dreadful to both people and king;

G, stands for George, may God give him wisdom and grace;

H, stands for hypocrite, who wears a double face.

J, stands for justice, which traitors in power defy,

K, stands for king, who should to such the axe apply;

L, stands for London, to its country ever true,

M, stands for Mansfield, who hath another view.

N, stands for North, who to the House the mandate brings,

O, stands for oaths, binding on subjects not on kings:

P, stands for people, who their freedom should defend,

Q, stands for quere, when will England's troubles end ?

R, stands for rebels, not at Boston but at home,

S, stands for Stuart, sent by Whigs abroad to roam,

T, stands for Tories, who may try to bring them back,

V, stands for villains, who have well deserved the rack.

W, stands for Wilkes, who us from warrants saved,

Y, for York, the New, half corrupted, half enslaved,

Z, stands for Zero, but means the Tory minions,

Who threatens us with fire and sword, to bias our opinions,

Stand firmly A and Z,

We swear, for ever to be free!

This document also available online at www.teachingthrough games.com for printing.

### Other Sources
*The American Revolution and the Young Republic: 1763 to 1816*
Written by Britannica Educational Publishing
Published by Britannica Educational Publishing, 2011
ISBN: 9781615306688

## Mini Reading Lesson

Read the lyrics to the ballad "Alphabet for Little Masters and Misses" and discuss the people and ideas presented for each letter. Many have been presented in prior lessons, others might need to be researched further. For example, Wilkes refers to John Wilkes, a member of the British Parliament who was supportive of the American colonies. It is also interesting to note that the lyrics of this song from 1775 do not speak of independence. In fact, the letter "I" is conspicuously absent from the alphabet. What message might the author have been sending by leaving the letter out?

Introduce the previous vocabulary. The words can be introduced even if they are not in the specific reading you have chosen.

## Guided Practice

Have students preview any headings and subheadings in the reading they have been asked to do. Have students read the selections.

### Read and Discuss

Have students reread each section of the text and discuss the following:

- What was the initial British counter-attack and how successful was it?
- Crossing the Delaware and Valley Forge are both symbols of the Revolutionary War. How do these two events present two different faces of the war?
- What groups were brought in to support both sides of the conflict? Why might the Native American group be considered a more volatile group that the other two groups?
- How were both sides ultimately "winners" in the Treaty of Paris?
- What problems were faced by the Americans as they sought to form their new country?

## MODEL

The "Alphabet for Little Masters and Misses" is an example of wartime propaganda; materials produced to illicit an emotional, often nationalistic, response in an audience. Paul Revere's engraving of the Boston Massacre was another example of patriot propaganda that distorted or exaggerated details to strengthen a particular viewpoint. You can share modern examples of wartime propaganda produced by the United States during the Second World War available online from the National Archives at http://www.archives.gov/exhibits/powers_of_persuasion/powers_of_persuasion_home.html.

The posters use a variety of methods to evoke strong emotional responses. Some posters feature exaggerated, menacing enemy figures threatening the United States or women and children. Others feature civilians or military personnel in heroic poses designed to suggest strength and resolve. Discussing the goals and methods of propaganda will help students understand how and why these materials are created and prepare them to create their own patriot themed propaganda in a re-write of parts of the "Alphabet for Little Masters and Misses."

## INDEPENDENT PRACTICE

Have students re-read the song lyrics of "Alphabet for Young Masters and Misses" and come up with replacement words for different letters. This can be done individually or in groups. Students should be able to explain and defend their choice of a new word.

### Writing Activities

**Narrative:** Choose the role of a Hessian soldier or a French soldier. Write a letter home to your family telling what you are doing, why, and how you feel about your actions.

**Inform or Explain:** Explain how the Battle of Saratoga, the winter spent at Valley Forge, and the events at Yorktown reflect the many faces of the American Revolutionary War.

**Express an Opinion:** Was the Treaty of Paris fair to both sides? Support your position.

## SHARING/REFLECTION

Have students share their new words for the alphabet song with the class. Publish a new broadside using the new vocabulary.

## ASSESSMENT

Review the re-written materials for "Alphabet for Little Masters and Misses." A well-executed re-write will focus on important people, places, and events from the American Revolution. In the style of propaganda, it will also use exaggeration to heavily promote the Patriot viewpoint.

## EXTENSION ACTIVITIES

**Further Research:** Research the role of one of the following people in war that are included in the game's various decks of cards: George Washington, Comte De Rochambeau, Benjamin Franklin, Betsy Ross, Louis XVI, the Queen's Rangers, and John Butler. Use the cards' short statements as a starting point.

**Timeline:** Find a timeline of the battles of the war and explore the connections between events. Summarize your findings focusing in part on the changing status of winners and losers.

# NOTES

1. A. M. Mood and R. D. Specht, *Gaming as a Technique of Analysis* (Santa Monica, CA: RAND Corporation, 1954).
2. Ibid.
3. Henry Wadsworth Longfellow. "Paul Revere's Ride."
4. Arthur Bernon Tourtellot, *Lexington and Concord: The Beginning of the War of the American Revolution* (New York, NY: W. W. Norton, 1963) p. 203.
5. MassHist.org, "The Examination of Doctor Franklin, before an August Assembly, relating to the Repeal of the Stamp-Act, &c," Retrieved July 2014 (http://www.masshist.org/revolution/doc-viewer.php?old=1&mode=nav&item_id=282).
6. Ibid.
7. Robert Middlekauff, *The Glorious Cause: The American Revolution, 1763–1789* (New York, NY: Oxford University Press, 2005) p. 116-117.
8. John K. Alexander, *Samuel Adams: America's Revolutionary Politician* (Lanham, MD: Rowman & Littlefield, 2002) p. 129.
9. Emerson, Ralph Waldo. "Concord Hymn." 1837.
10. Wikisource, "Declaration of the Causes and Necessity of Taking Up Arms," Retrieved July 2014 (http://en.wikisource.org/wiki/Declaration_of_the_Causes_and_Necessity_of_Taking_Up_Arms).
11. Ibid.
12. Allen, Thomas B., "Who Were the Tories?" Retrieved July 2014 (http://www.toriesfightingfortheking.com/WhoTories.htm).
13. Wikisource, "Common Sense," Retrieved July 2014 (http://en.wikisource.org/wiki/Common_Sense).
14. Ibid.
15. Wikisource, "Declaration of Independence," Retrieved July 2014 (http://en.wikisource.org/wiki/United_States_Declaration_of_Independence).
16. Ibid.

17. Ibid.
18. Ibid.
19. Isaacson, Walter, *Benjamin Franklin: An American Life* (New York, NY: Simon and Schuster, 2004) p. 317.

# APPENDIX 1

## COMMON CORE LEARNING STANDARDS

The following concepts from the Common Core State Standards are addressed in this unit:

### Reading Informational Texts Standards for Grades 6–8

Cite specific textual evidence to support analysis of primary and secondary sources.

- Determine the central ideas or information of a primary or secondary source; provide an accurate summary of the source distinct from prior knowledge or opinions.
- Identify key steps in a text's description of a process related to history/social studies (e.g., how a bill becomes law, how interest rates are raised or lowered).
- Determine the meaning of words and phrases as they are used in a text, including vocabulary specific to domains related to history/social studies.
- Describe how a text presents information (e.g., sequentially, comparatively, causally).
- Identify aspects of a text that reveal an author's point of view or purpose (e.g., loaded language, inclusion or avoidance of particular facts).
- Integrate visual information (e.g., in charts, graphs, photographs, videos, or maps) with other information in print and digital texts.
- Distinguish among fact, opinion, and reasoned judgment in a text.
- Analyze the relationship between a primary and secondary source on the same topic.

## Writing Standards for Grades 6–8

- Write arguments to support claims with clear reasons and relevant evidence.
- Write informative/explanatory texts to examine a topic and convey ideas, concepts, and information through the selection, organization, and analysis of relevant content.
- Write narratives to develop real or imagined experiences or events using effective technique, relevant descriptive details, and well-structured event sequences.
- Conduct short research projects to answer a question, drawing on several sources and refocusing the inquiry when appropriate.
- Gather relevant information from multiple print and digital sources, assess the credibility of each source, and quote or paraphrase the data and conclusions of others while avoiding plagiarism and providing basic bibliographic information for sources.
- Draw evidence from literary or informational texts to support analysis, reflection, and research.

## SOCIAL STUDIES STANDARDS

The four dimensions of informed inquiry included in the social studies framework for developing state standards are:

- Developing questions and planning inquiries.
- Applying disciplinary concepts and tools.
- Evaluating sources and using evidence.
- Communicating conclusions and taking informed action.

The lessons in this unit on the American Revolution allow students to meet the first three dimensions in the directed parts of the lessons and in the extension activities. The fourth dimension is only met in part because while they are asked to express an opinion, students are not asked to take informed action in these lesson.

The following content standards from the Framework for Social Studies State Standards are addressed within the unit:

## History

- D2.His.1.6–8. Analyze connections among events and developments in broader historical contexts.
- D2.His.2.6–8. Classify series of historical events and developments as examples of change and/or continuity.
- D2.His.3.6–8. Use questions generated about individuals and groups to analyze why they, and the developments they shaped, are seen as historically significant.
- D2.His.14.6–8. Explain multiple causes and effects of events and developments in the past.
- D2.His.15.6–8. Evaluate the relative influence of various causes of events and developments in the past.
- D2.His.16.6–8. Organize applicable evidence into a coherent argument about the past.

## Civics

- D2.Civ.8.6-8. Analyze ideas and principles contained in the founding documents of the United States, and explain how they influence the social and political system.
- D2.Civ.12.6-8. Assess specific rules and laws (both actual and proposed) as means of addressing public problems.
- D2.Civ.13.6-8. Analyze the purposes, implementation, and consequences of public policies in multiple settings.

# APPENDIX 2

## DATA GATHERING SHEETS

To access supplementary materials, go to http://www.teachingthrough-games.com. Then enter the code word **forliberty** in order to be directed to the following worksheets:

Important Details Worksheet

| | Important Detail | Reason Chosen |
|---|---|---|
| 1 | | |
| 2 | | |
| 3 | | |
| 4 | | |
| 5 | | |
| 6 | | |
| 7 | | |
| 8 | | |
| 9 | | |
| 10 | | |

# ABOUT THE AUTHORS

**Christopher Harris, Editorial Director** chris@playplaylearn.com
Chris is the director of a School Library System in western New York
that has provided a curriculum aligned board game library to member
school districts since 2007. His current position as a certified school
administrator, along with his background as a teacher, technology
coordinator, and school librarian have provided Chris with many different perspectives on gaming and learning. Being able to speak with
fellow administrators including principals and curriculum directors
about the value of board games as a part of teaching and learning has
been key to the success of the game library he founded as part of the
Genesee Valley Educational Partnership School Library System in
2007. Chris was a member of the National Expert Panel for the
American Library Association Gaming and Libraries grant in 2007-
2008 and has continued to present nationally on gaming in schools
and libraries as well as other school, technology and library topics.
He writes a monthly column in School Library Journal called "The
Next Big Thing" and co-authored *Libraries Got Game: Aligned Learning
through Modern Board Games* (ALA Editions, 2010) with Brian Mayer.

**Brian Mayer, Design & Development** brian@playplaylearn.com A
certified teacher and school librarian, Brian currently works as a gaming and library technology specialist for the Genesee Valley
Educational Partnership where, since 2007, he has curated and man-
aged a game library of over 300 curricularly aligned resources.
Working with school librarians and classroom teachers, Brian utilizes
game resources, design exercises and play experiences to help students engage with and find new meaning within the classroom
curriculum. Brian is a founding board member of American Library
Association's Games and Gaming Roundtable. Brian is the co-author
of *Libraries Got Game: Aligned Learning through Modern Board Games*
(ALA Editions, 2010). He has also written articles about gaming in
schools and libraries for School Library Journal and Knowledge

Quest, and presents and runs workshops at state and national conferences exploring the value of games and play for education and growth. In addition to this work, Brian is also the author of the game *Freedom: The Underground Railroad*, published by Academy Games in 2013. Freedom has gone on to win multiple awards and receive much critical acclaim.

**Dr. Patricia Harris, Curriculum & Instruction**  pat@playplay-learn.com After working more than 10 years in public schools both rural and urban and spending 8 years at an engineering school teaching social sciences, communication skills, and technology, Dr. Patricia Harris spent the last years of her career as head of an elementary education program, technology coordinator for the education department, and educational consultant for a physicians assistant graduate program. Her research and practical focus in education has been working with teachers at all grade levels, including working with an elementary teacher to co-teach a clinical class for several years, to build pedagogical strength. Dr. Harris's experience with social studies and science instructional methodology helps inform the curriculum alignment and classroom use scenarios presented here.

# NOTES

# NOTES

# NOTES

# NOTES

# NOTES

# NOTES